The Lavendon Collection of

BOBBIN LACE PATTERNS

The Lavendon Collection of
BOBBIN LACE PATTERNS

VALERIE HARRIS

DRYAD PRESS LTD
LONDON

Acknowledgment

I would like to thank all members of the Thameside and Wyvern Lacemakers for their help and encouragement, particularly Vera Wilks who typed my manuscript. Thanks are also due to Doreen Fudge of Luton Museum, and Sylvia Bull of the Cowper and Newton Museum, Olney, for their research.

Finally I must thank all members of my family for their assistance, especially Mum; Dad; Stan, who took the photographs; Rachel; Peter; and Mike, who did the drawing of the candlestand; for their love and support.

Fig. 20 is reproduced by kind permission of the *Malvern Gazette/Ledbury Reporter* and Fig. 21 by kind permission of the *Romford/Hornchurch Recorder*.

ISBN 0 8521 9649 0

Typeset by Servis Filmsetting Ltd, Manchester
and printed in Great Britain by
The Bath Press Ltd
Bath, Avon
for the publishers
Dryad Press Ltd
8 Cavendish Square
London W1M OAJ

CONTENTS

INTRODUCTION

In the summer of 1984 I inherited Maud Wooding's collection of lace, bobbins and prickings. Maud was my mother's cousin and she and her younger sister Betty, who died in 1980, had been lacemakers since they were children at the turn of the century. Together with their mother and elder sister Nellie, they had carried on the craft during the difficult years between the wars, and were among the few who passed it on, helping to keep the craft alive. They collected together many interesting things, many of which I felt should be shared with other lacemakers. 'Aunty Maudie' and 'Aunty Betty' were always happy to show their collection to anyone who was interested and had many visitors to their house in Malvern, Worcestershire. Now many other lacemakers will be able to enjoy it too.

Because lacemaking is usually, but not always, a feminine craft, the lacemakers in our family have no common surname. That is why I have called this collection of patterns 'The Lavendon Collection' – after the village where our lacemaking roots began, which also became the name of both my 'aunts'' house and my own.

Valerie Harris

ONE

A FAMILY OF
LACEMAKERS

Lavendon is the northernmost village in Buckinghamshire. It stands on the main A428 road midway between Bedford and Northampton. The nearest town is Olney, two miles to the south-west. Although only a moderate-sized village today, it was once a centre of some importance. The church, dedicated to St Michael, was founded before the Norman Conquest and still has it's Saxon tower, nave and chancel. There used to be a castle and an abbey, but the castle is now only a mound, and the abbey, founded in the twelfth century, disappeared in the reign of Henry VIII. The abbey moat is still there and some of the stones were said to have been used to build the Grange farm in 1625. This farmhouse was owned in the eighteenth century by Richard Newton, the founder of Hertford College, Oxford, and a kinsman of Sir Isaac Newton.

In the middle of the last century Lavendon was a lacemaking village. Its position at the junction of the three east-Midland lacemaking counties of Buckingham, Bedford and Northampton made this inevitable. My great-grandmother, Mary Barnes Pittams, was a lacemaker. She was born in 1841, and married my great-grandfather, John Odell, in 1862. They set up home in a cottage just out of the village along the Olney road. Their first daughter, Mary Elizabeth, was born in 1865, and my grandmother, Hannah Sophia, in 1867. There were other babies but they did not survive infancy.

From the stories that have been passed down to us it appears that Mary Elizabeth, usually known as Lizzie, was the sober, industrious daughter, while Hannah was more vivacious and fun-loving. However, they were great friends and remained close throughout their lives.

Mary Barnes Pittams had been taught to make lace at the age of four, and her daughters were only a little older when they started to attend lace school. They went for half a day; the other half being spent at the ordinary village school for a fee of 1d a week.

Their mother made Bucks Point lace at village group meetings. To these meetings she took a glass flask, filled with spring water. These flasks, or flashes, were placed in a special stand so that the light of a single candle could be diffused and used by as many people as possible.

Lizzie and Hannah learnt to make the new Bedford Maltese lace which was considered much more fashionable. They hardly ever made Bucks Point.

FIG 1. *Lavendon, Buckinghamshire, at the end of the nineteenth century*

FIG 2. *Mary Barnes Odell (née Pittams) aged 45*

FIG 3. *Hannah Sophia Odell, aged 18*

FIG 4. *Mary Elizabeth Odell (Lizzie) aged 20*

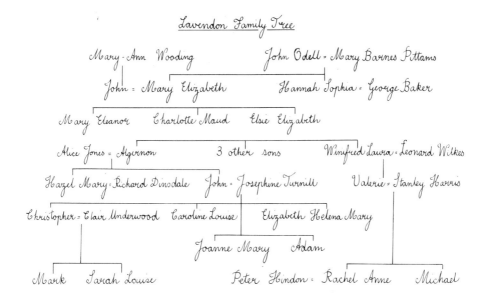

FIG 5. *The Lavendon family tree*

FIG 6.   *The flask, with its rush basket, that belonged to Mary Barnes Pittams. The water inside the flask is still clear*

FIG 7.   *A candle stand. The light from one candle could be used by many people*

FIG 8. *John Wooding in his postman's uniform*

The lace school was run by Mary-Ann Wooding. Lizzie became friendly with the teacher's son, John, and they married in 1889. He was a postman and after their marriage he found work at the General Post Office in Malvern, Worcestershire. It was here that their three daughters; Mary Eleanor, Charlotte Maud, and Elsie Elizabeth were born in 1890, 1891 and 1894 respectively. Shortly after this they moved to a more spacious house in North Malvern which they named after their native village. 'Lavendon' was always a warm, friendly house with an open door. Old-fashioned but full of charm and interesting things.

In 1909 John and Mary Odell moved to Malvern to live with Lizzie and her family. It was here that they celebrated their Golden Wedding in 1912. For .

FIG 9. *The Wooding sisters in 1912. Mary Eleanor (Nellie) standing, Elsie Elizabeth (Betty) with cat, and Charlotte Maud (Maudie)*

the occasion lace bobbins were made for all the female members of the family and a special pair for the couple themselves.

Mary Odell died in 1917, aged 76; her husband lived to the age of 85, dying in 1920.

Meanwhile their daughter Hannah had married in 1891. The family normally worshipped at the Union Chapel in Lavendon, but often visited the Baptist Church in Olney and it was here that Hannah met George Baker.

FIG 10. *Golden wedding photograph of John and Mary Odell with the bobbins that were made for the occasion*

Many lacemakers were non-conformists being descendants of the Huguenots who fled here from persecution in France in the sixteenth century.

George had been born in Buckden, Huntingdonshire (now part of Cambridgeshire) in 1868 and worked as a farm labourer after leaving school.

FIG 11. *Hannah Odell wearing her engagement ring in 1890*

FIG 12. *George Baker in his railwayman's uniform*

He joined the Midland Railway at the age of 19 as a platform porter at Thrapstone Station North. He also worked at Finedon Station, Northamptonshire, before coming to Olney in July 1889 as a signalman. He only stayed in the area for eight months but Hannah must have made an instant impression on him for after leaving to work in Didsbury, near Manchester, and Bedford, he returned to marry her in September, 1891. They married in Olney Baptist Church as the Lavendon Union Chapel was not at that time licensed for marriages.

George Baker's employment took him to many Midland towns and he finally became the chief signalman at Kings Heath Station, Birmingham, in

FIG 13. *Hannah Baker at her pillow in later life*

June 1899. Hannah had four sons, Herbert, Algernon, Oswald and Reginald, and then in 1906 my mother, Winifred Laura, was born. Looking after four boys kept her too busy to teach my mother to make lace, or so she said. I can remember her working on her pillow when she was an old lady and I have yet to see anyone who could work as fast.

Lizzie, however, had taught her three daughters and they all continued to make lace throughout the first half of this century at a time when the art almost died out. Many times they received bobbins, patterns and pillows from the families of lacemakers who had died. I have a bobbin winder with this signed

FIG 14. *A bobbin winder. The thread came in skeins which were placed over the pegs*

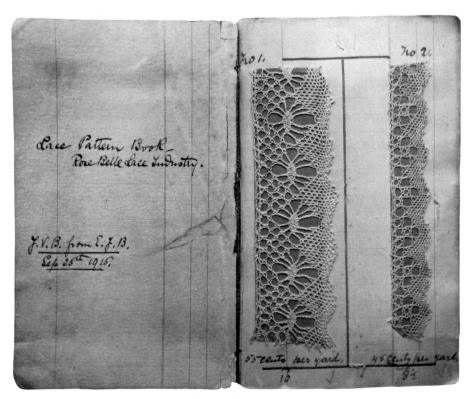

FIG 15. *The sample book of the Rose Belle Lace Industry*

FIG 16. *Betty Wooding at her pillow in the 1920s*

note in the drawer, 'I should like this bobing wheel to be given to the Woodings at Malvern has I have promised it them' (*sic*).

They also received the *Lace Pattern Book* of the Rose Belle Lace Industry, dated September, 1915. The samples are priced between 6d and 2/- per yard, and are mainly of Torchon design. As they also have French prices marked I think that it must have belonged to a lady called Katie Bagley, as there are also some patterns marked with her name stating the number of *fuseaux* needed. Three of these are included in the collection.

The eldest daughter, Mary Eleanor, always known as Nellie, tragically died of a sudden heart attack while still in her early fifties.

Maudie the second sister was an assistant in an haberdashers and later worked for some time at St James's Girls' School in West Malvern. Together with her mother and her sister Betty, who worked from home as a dressmaker, she made a great deal of lace. Betty used it to trim many of the dresses she made. She loved to design and would have liked to go to art college, but her parents did not approve of the idea. Her most popular lace designs were 'modesty vests' which were used frequently in the 1920s and 30s to fill in the necks of low-cut dresses. She also made motifs which were used as inserts on blouses and dresses.

One unusual request for a design came from a man who wanted a lace cover for his handmade shuttlecocks. However, he eventually decided that this was not a commercial proposition.

FIG 17. *Lizzie Wooding in later life. Notice
her large pillow*

    For many years one or other of the family demonstrated at the Three
Counties Show held annually in Malvern.

    In 1931 Lizzie Wooding received a letter from the Leicester School of
Stitchery and Lace which read as follows:

Dear Mrs. Wooding,

    Miss Sweet has asked me to write to you about your lace. I have put the prices that we
can pay against each of them and we should be very glad if you would make us one dozen
yards of the one at 1/8.

    We have an order on hand at present for night-gowns for the Queen and she has chosen
the fan lace and insertions to trim them. It is a big order as we are doing knickers as well,
– 1 dozen of each, so of course it will be impossible for one worker to do all the lace for
them, and we were wondering if you could do some of it. It is made with 150 linen. We
are having some more pricking done and if you would care to undertake any of the
insertions I would send a pricking to you as soon as they are done. We give 1/2d for the
insertion. Will you please let me have a card to say if you will make some and also
whether I shall send any 150. We should want $7\frac{1}{4}$ yards to start with as that does two
nightgowns.

Yours truly,
H. M. Dawes

The Queen referred to was, of course, Queen Mary. Lizzie agreed to do the
lace and a week later came the following letter:

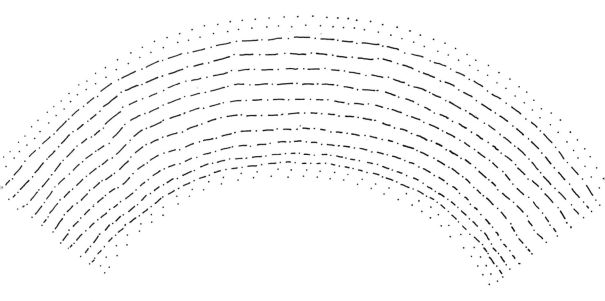

FIG 18. *Design for a lace cover for a*
shuttlecock. No instructions are available as to
how it should be worked!

Dear Mrs. Wooding,

   I am so glad that you can do this insertion for us. I find it is 100 linen not 150 but I am
sending it just the same and if you have any by you this can be returned when you send
the lace – we give 1/2 for it.

Yours truly,
H. M. Dawes

Four weeks later she wrote:

Dear Mrs. Wooding,

   I do hope that the 7¼ yards of insertion is nearly done as our worker is waiting to get on
with the Queen's nightgowns until she has it. I should be very glad of it as soon as
possible.

Yours truly,
H. M. Dawes

It was then that Betty discovered that her mother had been wrongly charged
for some thread and obviously wrote very strongly to the school about that and
also the poor remuneration given. She received this reply:

Dear Miss Wooding,

   There was a mistake about the quantity of thread sent to your mother and we are so
sorry about it and now enclose the 2/1 which should have been added to the 3/9 – the fact
is Miss Dawes lost her father just at the end of April and the family home had to be
broken up so, as you may imagine, her thoughts were not entirely on her work and its not
surprising that mistakes were made. The thread put down to you we find should have

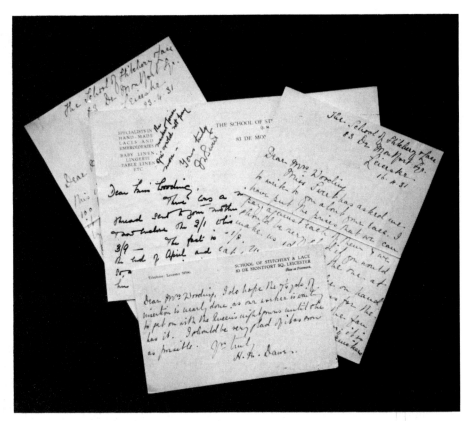

FIG 19. *Letters sent by the School of Lace and Stitchery*

been on the line immediately below against another workers name.

All workers find their own thread, not only working for us but for every other industry I have ever come across, and no-one had ever expected otherwise in all the 10 years that we have employed others.

I quite agree that lace is appallingly badly paid but if we were to give more we could never sell it – foreign lace or machine lace would be used instead, and it must be remembered that it is a spare-time occupation and can be done by invalids or old people who could not otherwise earn anything at all! – of course with your mother it is different. Although the lace is for the Queen she knows exactly the market price of it and would not pay more –

Yours truly,
J. W. Sweet

When Betty read this she refused to let her mother continue with her work so I am afraid that our family cannot claim to have made lace for members of the royal family.

However, Lizzie continued making lace until she died in 1947, four years after her husband John.

FIG 20. *Betty Wooding demonstrating lacemaking*

FIG 21. *Rachel Harris, aged 10, demonstrating at a craft fair*

As my mother had never learnt to make lace she wanted me to have the opportunity to do so. My grandmother felt that she would not be able to work slowly enough to teach me, so when I was 11 I went to stay at Malvern in order to have lessons from Maudie and Betty. I was given my own child's-size bolster pillow, some plain wooden bobbins and the choice of a few old bone ones. The aunts also gave a set to my daughter Rachel when she learnt at the age of eight.

All the bobbins and patterns have now been passed on to me. Betty died in 1980 and Maudie in 1984. They were the kindest and most charming of ladies each having a strong sense of humour and a firm faith in God.

As their home has had to be sold we have now called our house 'Lavendon'.

THE
PATTERNS

Apart from the last five, which are my own designs, the following patterns all belonged to Maudie and Betty Wooding. Some were passed on to them through the family, some came from other lacemakers, still more they designed themselves.

They are presented in rough chronological order, from the Bucks Point prickings of Mary Barnes Pittams, through Bedford Maltese and Torchon to my own modern lace.

I have divided the patterns into five sections according to their original owners. Each section includes some easy patterns for beginners, and others more advanced. Where I have them, I have included illustrations of samples of the lace, but occasionally there is a pricking on its own as a challenge to the more experienced lacemakers. Very few of the patterns have been 'trued' and the majority of them have their original markings.

The original prickings were made on a variety of materials; some on old vellum parchment with cloth attached in order to hold the pins; some on rather battered cardboard; and others on scraps of paper.

The names of the patterns are family names; names appearing on old bobbins in my possession or the names of places with family connections.

In the larger patterns, which have had to be divided, the join is marked by corresponding alphabetical letters.

T W O

GREAT-GRANDMOTHER'S PATTERNS

(4 Bucks Point patterns)

A great deal of my great-grandmother's Bucks Point lace has not survived, but I do have two handkerchiefs from a set that she made for all the ladies in the family, having had the linen handkerchiefs especially sent from Ireland. All the lace for these was made in a simple design of rings and diamonds.

Of the four patterns included, only one has a sample of the lace. I hope that the other prickings provide a welcome challenge to experienced lacemakers.

They are all copied exactly from the original prickings. Their names as many will realise, come from mottoes on old lace bobbins.

Pattern one – *I love the boys* (edging)
This rather broad Bucks Point design has swirls of cloth stitch with just one small area of honeycomb filling. As previously mentioned the pricking has been copied exactly – warts and all!

In the original, each repeat of the pattern is slightly different.

The old stained vellum parchment has a cloth-strip at each end to hold the pins.

The lace in the sample has been incorporated into a modesty vest. This was used to fill in the low necks of dresses and was usually attached with press-studs or small gold safety pins.

The name of the pattern is a very popular old bobbin motto.

Pattern two – *Love me truley* (sic) (edging)
This is another old Bucks Point pattern on old vellum. There is no surviving sample of the lace but it is relatively simple. The filling is whole-stitch cucumber.

The name is taken exactly from an old bobbin. I am afraid that spelling was not always a bobbin-maker's strong point!

Pattern three – *Love, forget-me-not* (edging)
This delicate Bucks Point pattern with its ground dotted with square tallies has clover leaves in cloth-stitch, and tiny flowers outlined with a gimp. As there is no surviving sample of the lace, I leave it to the lacemaker to work out where the gimp goes.

The original pricking is on an unusually pale parchment that is almost white in colour.

Pattern four – *Marry-me-quick* (edging)
This is the only one of the four Bucks Point edgings whose original pricking is on glazed card rather than parchment; obviously it is a slightly more modern design.

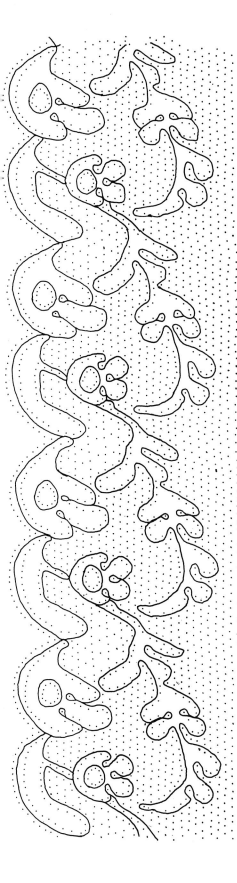

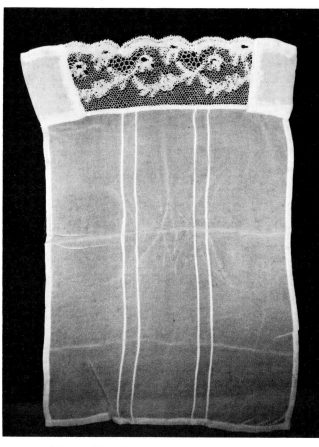

FIG 22.   *Pattern 1 I love the boys*

FIG 23.   *Pricking for pattern 1* I love the boys

FIG 24. *Pricking for pattern 2* Love me truely (sic)

FIG 25. *Pricking for pattern 3* Love, forget-me-not

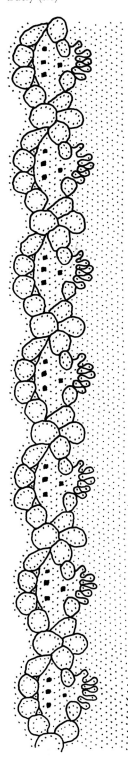

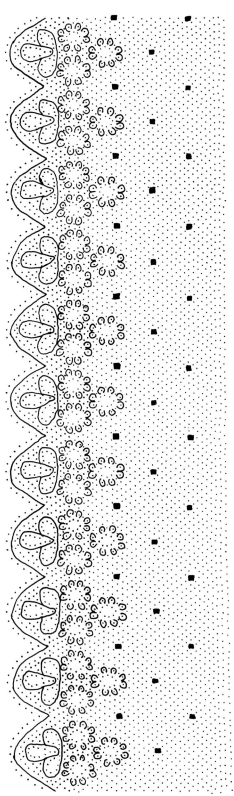

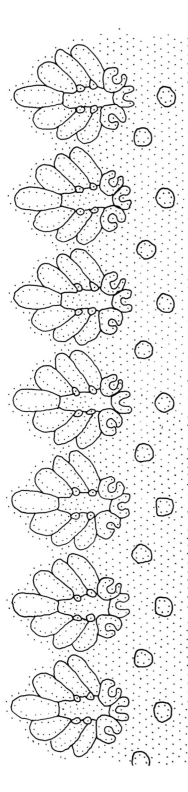

FIG 26. *Pricking for pattern 4* Marry me
quick

27

THREE

GRANDMOTHER'S PATTERNS

(31 Bedford Maltese patterns)

My grandmother, Hannah Sophia Baker, and her sister, Mary Elizabeth Wooding, made a huge amount of Bedford Maltese lace in their life-times. In their day Bucks Point Lace was considered very old-fashioned.

They used bolster pillows much larger than the ones in present use. The average width was at least 19 inches with a diameter of 11 inches. The pillow on which I was taught was considered a child's size at 14 inches wide by nine inches diameter.

These larger pillows enabled the worker to make wide lace, such as tablecloth edgings and dress flounces, more easily. Collars, too, very fashionable at the turn of the century, were much more easily made on the broader pillows. The pillows were balanced on the knee and rested on a wooden stand called a 'horse'.

I believe that Hannah and Lizzie must have worked at some time for the Bucks Cottage Workers' Agency, set up in Olney in the early years of this century. Many of their prickings are for lace featured in the B.C.W.A. catalogue. The Agency exported lace to many countries and won the Gold Medal at the Festival of Empire and Imperial Exhibition in 1911.

Pattern one – *Lavendon* (collar)
The original pricking for this collar is on parchment and very old. Although it comes from my family's collection, I have the feeling that it could be a foreign pattern as it is marked out in the opposite way to all the other collars. It has the unusual feature of tallies incorporated into a nine-pin type edging.

As with all large collars, the pattern should be started at the rounded end, and worked to the centre. The work should then be removed from the pillow, turned over and the last repeat of the pattern pinned back in place. Then work back to the beginning.

28

FIG 27. *Pattern 1* Lavendon *collar*

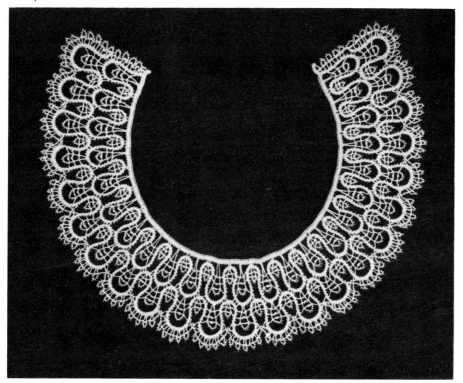

FIG 28. *Pattern 1* Lavendon *detail*

FIG 29. *Pricking for pattern 1* Lavendon
part I

A ——————— ————— B

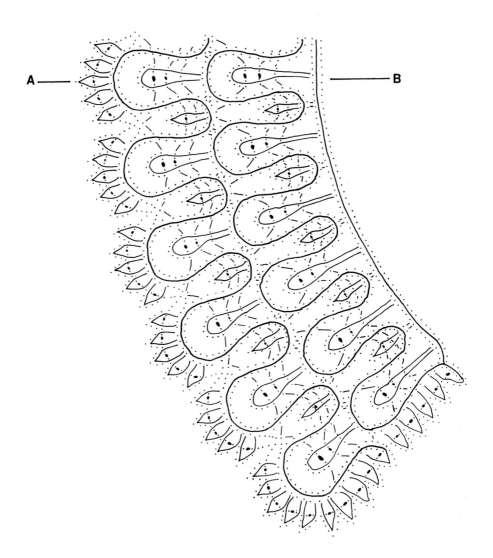

FIG 30. *Pricking for pattern 1* Lavendon
part II

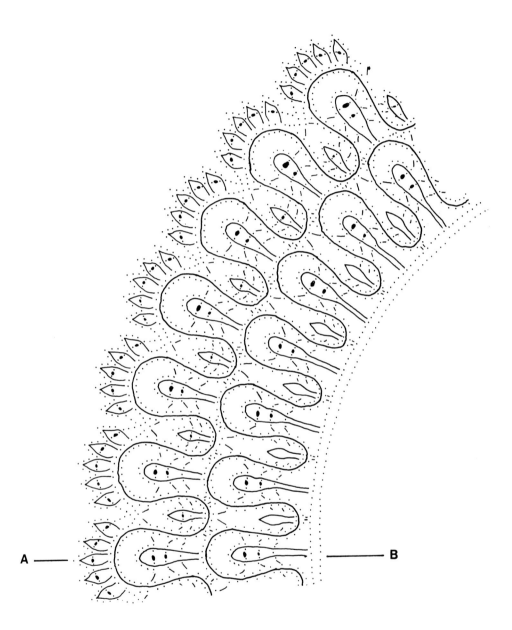

A ———   ——— B

FIG 31. *Pattern 2* Mary Barnes *collar*

Pattern two – *Mary Barnes* (collar)

This too is a very old pattern; the lace sample is over one hundred years old and rather worn in places. The design is a typical Bedford Maltese one with a nine-pin edge both sides, tallies arranged in a leaf design and whole-stitch flowers. Note that the tallies are made the traditional English way with square ends. The sample was made in a soft cotton thread which was called 'slip'.

The collar could almost be the one that Lizzie Odell is wearing in Fig. 4. This style of neckware had the advantage of being worn either way round.

FIG 32. *Pattern 2* Mary Barnes *detail*

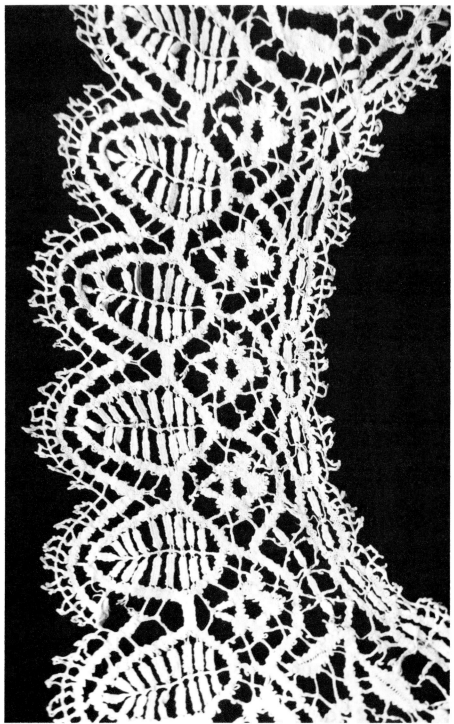

FIG 33. *Pricking for pattern 2* Mary Barnes
part I

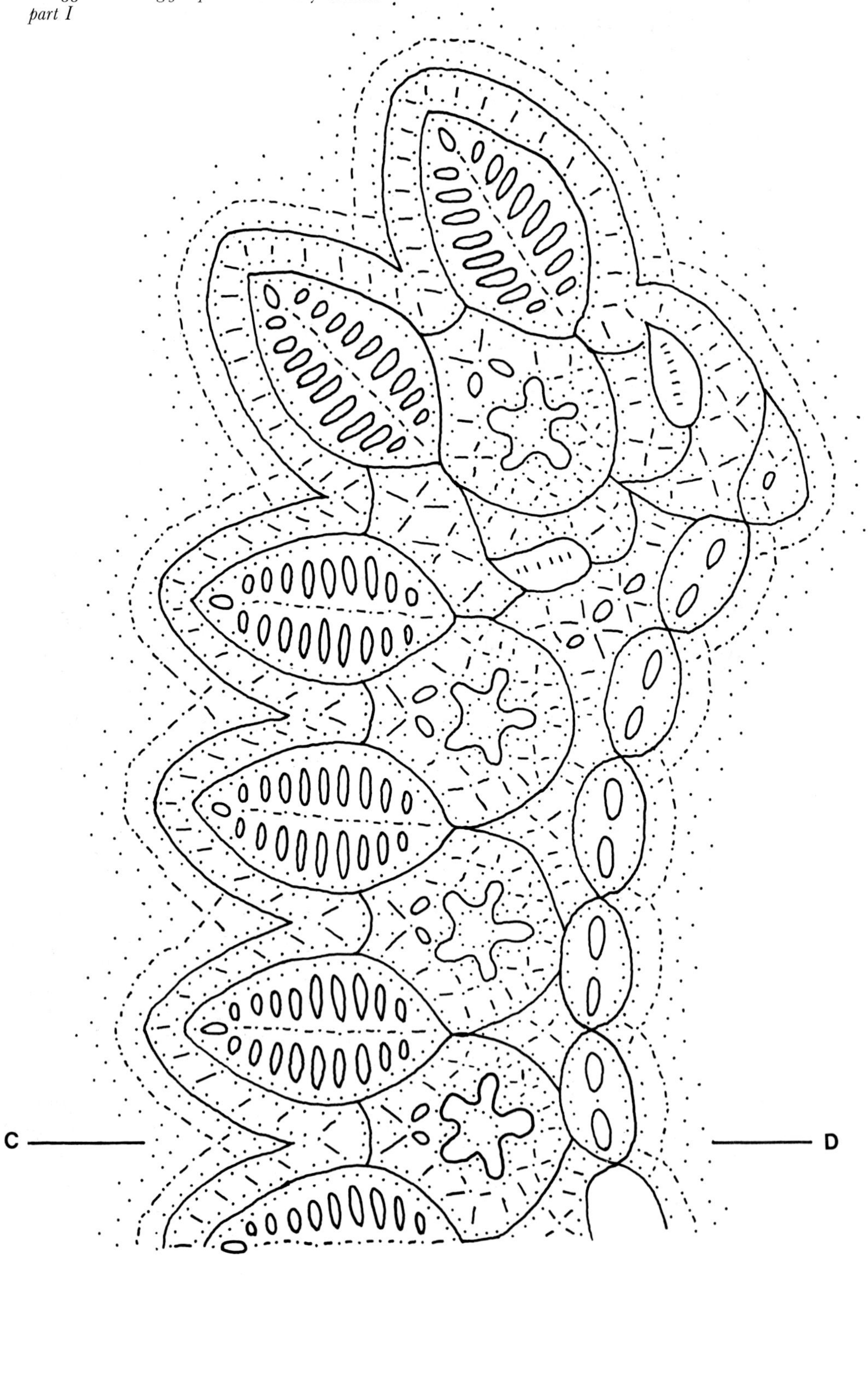

C ———————— D

FIG 34. *Pricking for pattern 2* Mary Barnes *part II*

D

FIG 35. *Pattern 3* Edith *collar*

Pattern three – *Edith* (collar and cuffs)
This collar and cuff pattern must have been a very popular design at the end of the last century. I have three samples of it in the family collection and its original pricking is probably the most well-worn of all the prickings. For this reason I am afraid that it is rather inaccurate in places. At one time a nine-pin border was added on the inside edge, but I have omitted this as it is obviously not original, having been pricked out over some wording.

The starting point is suggested on the original pricking. For the collar work the pattern completely, turn the work over, set the last head up again and work back to the start. For a matching cuff work four heads, turn and set up again. Work three heads back making seven heads in all.

36

FIG 36. *Pricking for pattern 3* Edith *part I*

Commence here

E———

———F

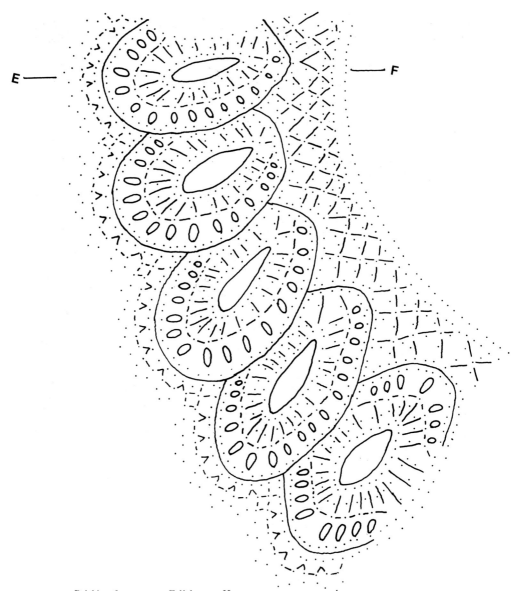

E —— F

FIG 37. *Pricking for pattern 3* Edith *part II*

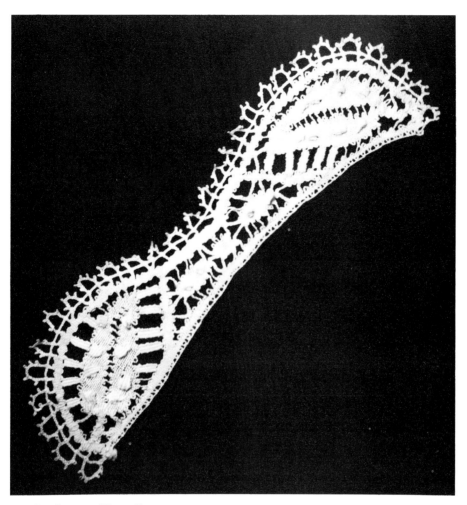

FIG 38. *Pattern 4* Alice *collar*

Pattern four – *Alice* (collar)
This little half collar is based on one of the designs featured in the Bucks Cottage Workers' Agency catalogue. In the catalogue there are three half stitch buds rather than the whole stitch ones with raised tallies. The price for the collar was 1/4d. Whoever made the family sample – probably Lizzie Wooding – forgot to work tallies in the upper right-hand corner.

The mark X on the pricking indicates a 'kiss' (*see glossary*).

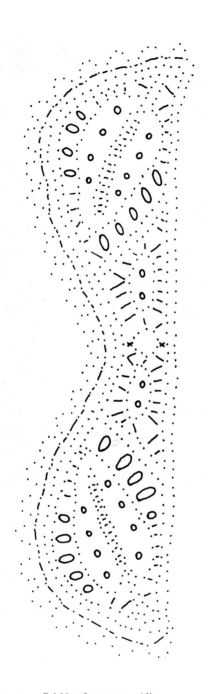

FIG 39. *Pricking for pattern 4* Alice

FIG 40. *Pattern 5* Sally *collar*

Pattern five – *Sally* (collar)

This is another collar from the Bucks Cottage Workers' Agency catalogue, although once again there is a slight difference. There are extra tallies round the edge of the outer leaves in the catalogue collar, which is priced at 2/-.

These half collars, often made for children's dresses, were sometimes called Peter Pan collars. If the two halves were joined by a narrow band of lace it was known as a stock collar.

41

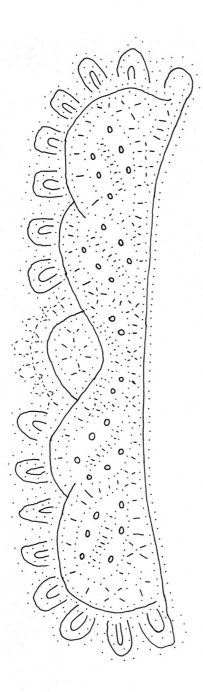

Pattern six – *Helena* (collar or camisole top)

The original of this pricking is rather scrappy and very roughly marked, I have included it because it is an interesting example of the type of collar. It is made with very coarse thread and styled almost like a yoke, so it could have been used as a camisole top. Both the buds and the trail are made in half stitch. The pricking must have been sent to my grandmother to make for an order as it has her name written on it.

FIG 41. *Pricking for pattern 5* Sally

FIG 42. *Pattern 6* Helena *collar*

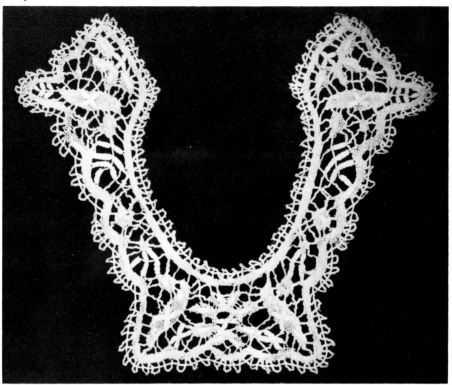

FIG 43. *Pattern 6* Helena *detail*

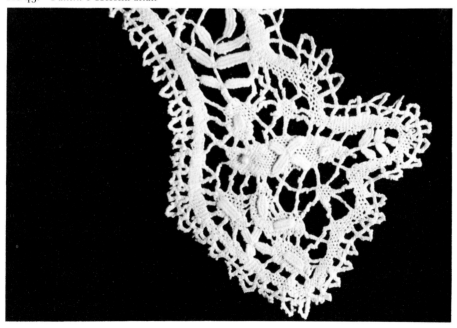

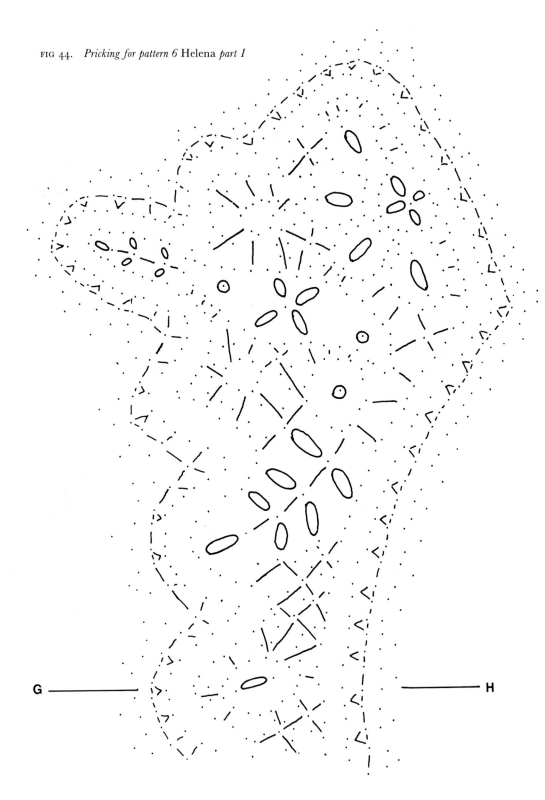

FIG 44. *Pricking for pattern 6* Helena *part I*

G ———————— | ————————— H

FIG 45. *Pricking for pattern 6* Helena *part II*

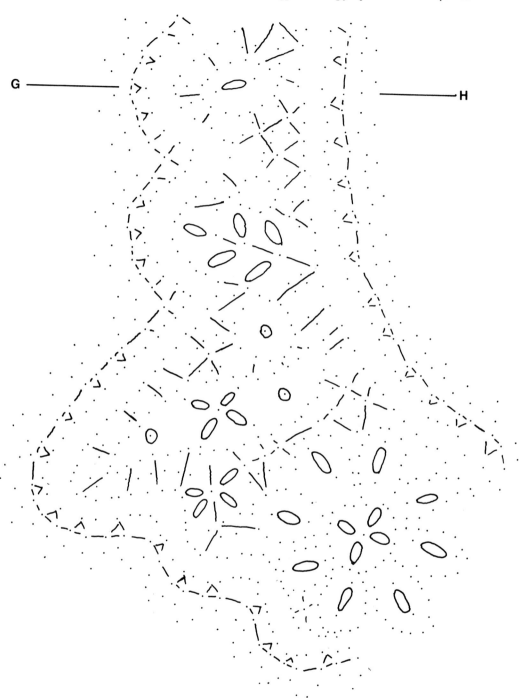

G ———————— H

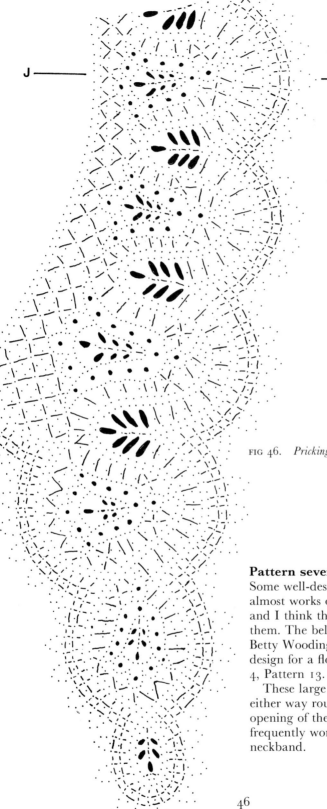

J —————   ————— K

FIG 46.   *Pricking for pattern 7* Olney *part I*

Pattern seven – *Olney* (collar)
Some well-designed lace prickings are
almost works of art in their own right
and I think that this is definitely one of
them. The bell-like motif was used by
Betty Wooding as the centre of her
design for a flower petal – see Chapter
4, Pattern 13.

These large collars could be worn
either way round according to the
opening of the dress. They were
frequently worn in conjunction with a
neckband.

K —————— J

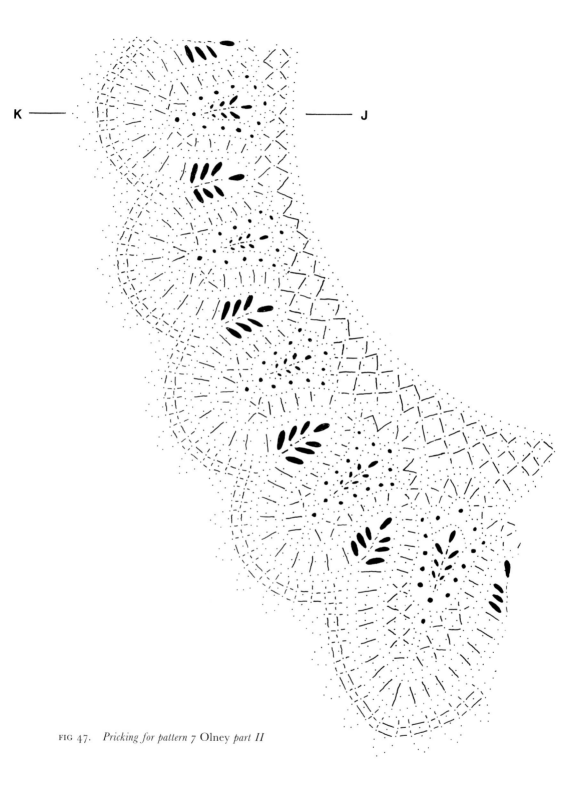

FIG 47.   *Pricking for pattern 7* Olney *part II*

47

FIG 48. *Pricking for pattern 8* Annie *part I*

L ——— M

48

FIG 49. *Pricking for pattern 8* Annie *part II*

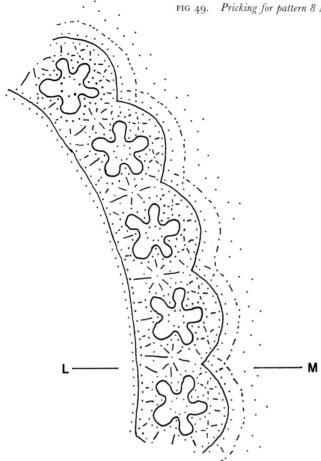

L——————————M

Pattern eight – *Annie* (collar)
This attractive little fall collar dates
from the end of the nineteenth century.
Its pricking is interesting in that it has
markings on both sides. Presumably
the pricking was turned over half-way
through the work rather than the more
usual method of turning over the lace.

It is likely that the daisy-like flowers
would have been outlined with a gimp
thread.

49

FIG 50. *Pricking for pattern 9* Victoria *part I*

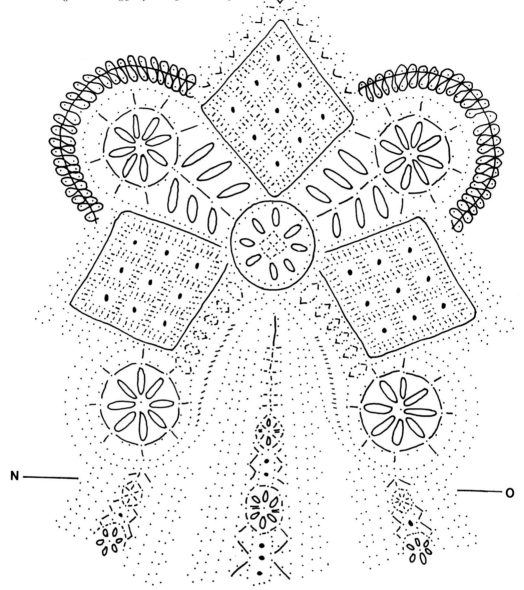

N ———

——— O

Pattern nine – *Victoria* (?)
This is a mystery pattern. I am uncertain as to what the finished lace was intended to be. Although it is a little small it could have been a head-dress. Alternatively it was, perhaps, meant to be worn as a jabot, or gathered together a little as a lace corsage. From the condition of the pricking I would think that it is the oldest pattern in my grandmother's collection.

50

FIG 51. *Pricking for pattern 9* Victoria *part II*

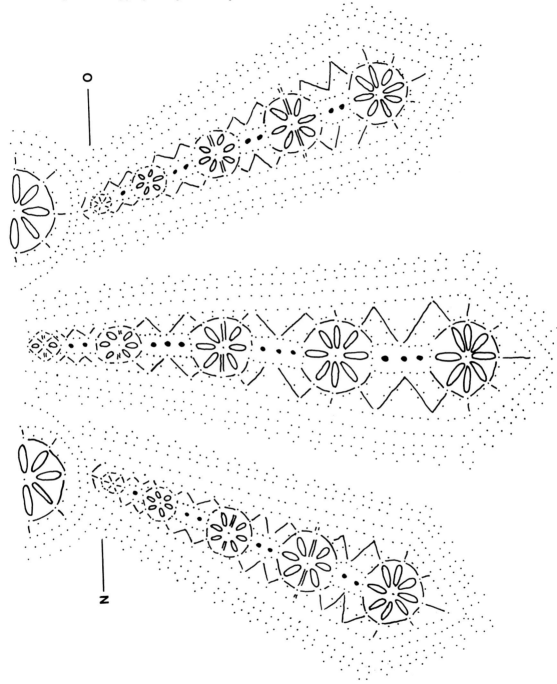

51

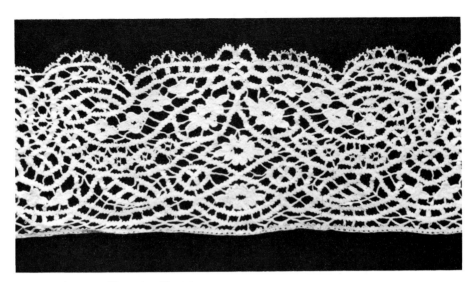

FIG 52. *Pattern 10* Hannah *wide edging*

Pattern ten – *Hannah* (wide edging)
This is another pattern whose pricking
is a work of art. It is a wide Bedford
Maltese edging which was a very
popular design judging by the amount
of it in the family collection. The lace
in the picture was made in a fine
cotton, although silk was also used.
The flower shapes are outlined with a
gimp. This lace would have been used
in flounces to trim ballgowns and
afternoon dresses.

FIG 53. *Pricking for pattern 10* Hannah

Pattern eleven – *Mary-Ann* (wide edging)

This wide Bedford Maltese edging holds a special place in the family history. As girls, Lizzie and Hannah had to fulfil a rush order in this design. It was for a ballgown to be worn at a special ball and in order to complete the lace they had to work in shifts through the day and night. Their lace work had the same tension so it could not be detected where one had finished and the other started. There is no sample of the lace. It is likely that when the ballgown was completed they never felt like making that pattern again!

The pricking shows two complete repeats of the pattern.

FIG 54. *Pricking for pattern 11* Mary-Ann *wide edging*

FIG 55. *Pattern 12* Lizzie *wide edging*

Pattern twelve – *Lizzie* (wide edging)
There is a mixture of Bedford Maltese and Bucks Point techniques in this wide pattern. The main ground consists of whole stitch buds linked by braids with picots, whereas that between the trails is Bucks Point ground with a spot or small tally in the centre. The wheatear design of tallies has always been popular as a fertility symbol.

There is a similar but narrower design in the Bucks Cottage Worker's Agency catalogue priced from 2/9d to 3/- a yard.

FIG 56. *Pricking for pattern 12* Lizzie

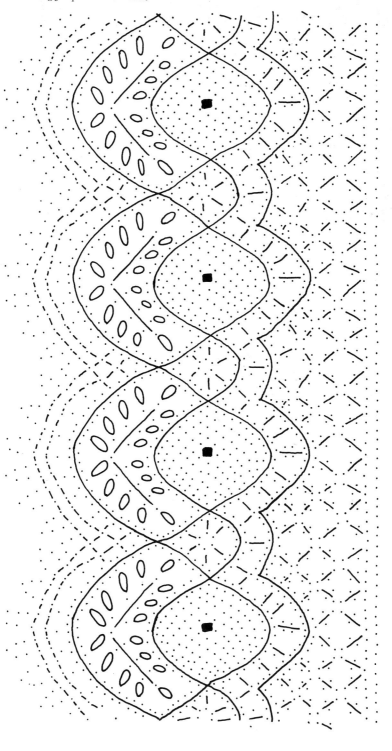

FIG 57. *Pattern 13* Ruth *edging*

Pattern thirteen – *Ruth* (edging)
This is a rather unusual edging. The
ground appears to be a variation of
honeycomb made with whole stitches.
Then there is the odd feature of the
hole at the base of the design although
this could have been used to thread a
ribbon for gathering.

The sample is in a fine linen with a
gimp outlining the petal shape.

The pricking has not been used a
great deal as it still has its original
markings all clearly visible.

FIG 58. *Pricking for pattern 13* Ruth

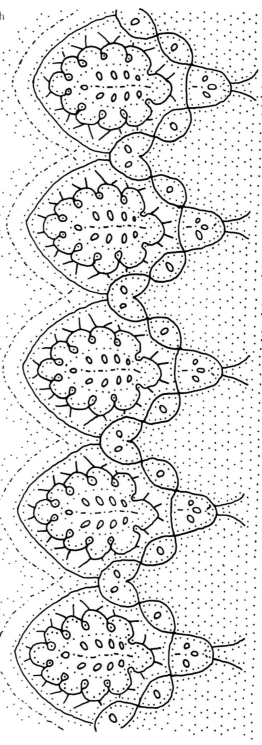

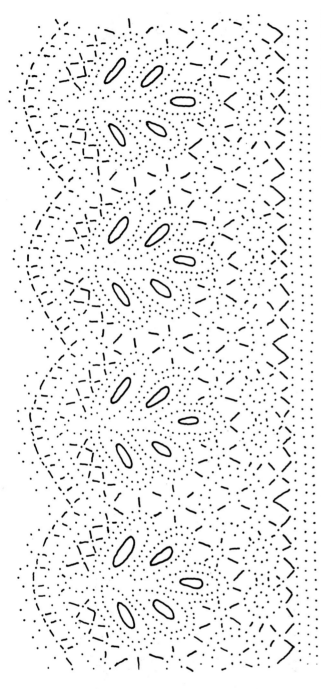

Pattern fourteen – *Susannah* (edging)
I have no sample available of this edging so it is possible that it was a pattern that my grandmother never got round to making. Once again the markings on the vellum pricking are all clearly visible.

I think that an experienced lacemaker would be able to work out the pattern for herself.

FIG 59. *Pricking for pattern 14* Susannah *edging*

Pattern fifteen – *Betsy* (edging)
This is one of the many variations of the basic Sunflower Bedford Maltese pattern which is sometimes known as the Wheel. The lace in the sample, probably used for one of my aunts' many modesty vests, is made in a very fine linen thread.

Note that where the double lines are marked on the pricking, the workers from the nearby trail or bud are twisted, used to make a join and then twisted again before returning to where they started.

FIG 60. *Pattern 15* Betsy *edging*

61

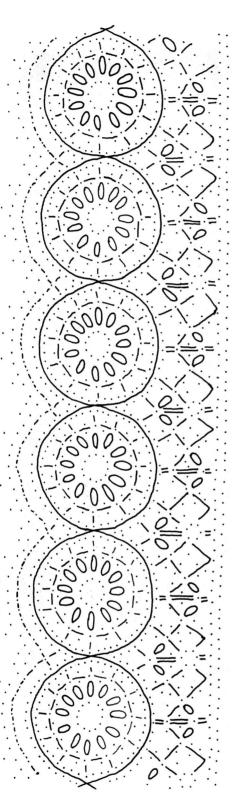

FIG 61. *Pricking for pattern 15* Betsy

Pattern sixteen – *Jane* (edging)
Another variation of a classic Bedford
Maltese design, this one is often known
as Running River. The original
pricking has been used too many times
for pricking out and as a result the
pinholes are far too large to hold the
pins properly.

Note that in the heads which do not
have tallies there is a horizontal braid
with a twisted pair on either side (not
always sufficiently twisted in the
sample!). These cross with a windmill
in the centre.

FIG 62.   *Pattern 16* Jane *edging*

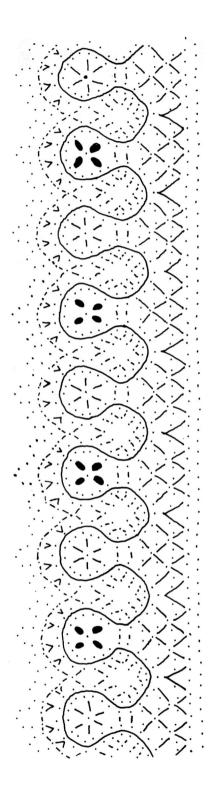

FIG 63. *Pricking for pattern 16* Jane

FIG 64. *Pattern 17* Louise *edging*

Pattern seventeen – *Louise* (edging)
Another variation of the Bedford
Maltese Sunflower design this time
alternating with a flower outlined by a
gimp. The original pricking is rather
casually drawn up. The number of
picots varies on the nine-pin edge and
in the ground. I have included it
because, judging by the well-worn
pricking, it was a very popular design.

Note the rather unusual way that
the nine-pin edge joins the trail. This is
quite common on older patterns.

The sample is in silk on a modesty
vest which also has lace insertions of a
very simple design. The workers from
the two footsides cross regularly with a
'kiss'.

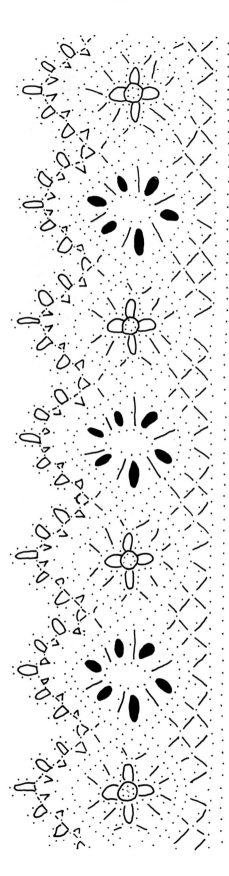

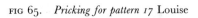
FIG 65. *Pricking for pattern 17* Louise

66

FIG 66. *Pattern 18* Frances *edging with corner*

Pattern eighteen – *Frances* (edging with corner)
Yet another variation of the Sunflower design, this was a favourite pattern for small tablecloths used for afternoon tea. A similar design appears in the Bucks Cottage Worker's Agency catalogue. A complete tablecloth cost 13/6d.

The sample here comes from a series that Maudie and Betty Wooding made to help customers choose when ordering lace. The thread is a linen of about 70 thickness. Note that a false tally is used at the top and bottom of the flower. This was often done by professional lacemakers to save the bother of adding extra pairs, when an odd number of tallies were to be made.

FIG 67. *Pricking for pattern 18* Frances

FIG 68. *Pattern 19* Martha *edging*

Pattern nineteen – *Martha* (edging)
An attractive neat Bedford Maltese edging that would have been used for trimming blouses and linen. The marking on the pricking has been copied exactly from the original and the lacemaker can decide if she agrees with the working in the sample.

It is unusual for the nine-pin edge to have only four picots on each head.

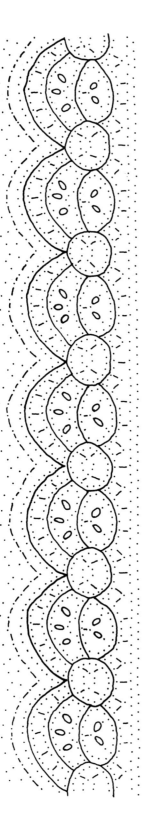

FIG 69. *Pricking for pattern 19* Martha

Pattern twenty – *Kitty* (edging)
This simple little Bedford Maltese
edging is unusual in having no nine-
pin edge, but notice that there are
picots on the headside. It may be that
it was designed by one of the family.
They made a great deal of it to trim
blouses and underwear.

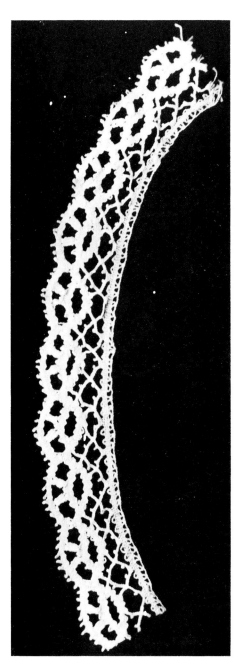

FIG 70. *Pattern 20* Kitty *edging*

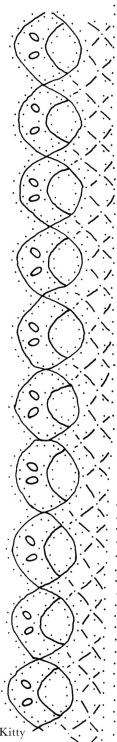

FIG 71. *Pricking for pattern 20* Kitty

71

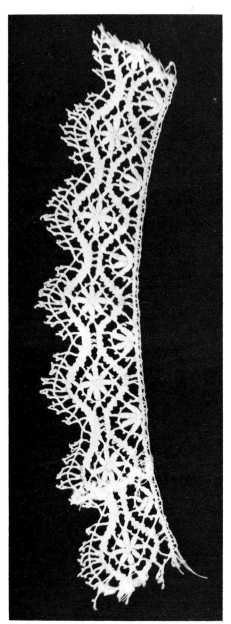

FIG 72. *Pattern 21 Susan edging*

Pattern twenty-one – *Susan* (edging)
The original pricking for this neat Bedford Maltese edging is on a very fine parchment that is almost transparent. In the sample you can see the rather rough way that joins were made between two pieces of lace.

Notice that 'kisses' rather than braids have been used between the two trails and again between the trail and the footbraid.

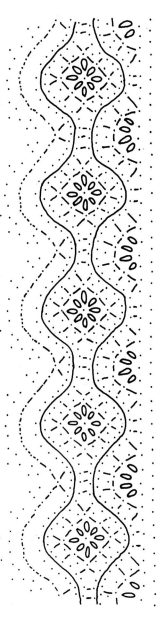

FIG 73. *Pricking for pattern 21 Susan*

FIG 74. *Pattern 22* Lucy *edging*

Pattern twenty-two – *Lucy* (edging)
A rather unusual asymmetric version of
the Bedford Maltese fertility pattern.
The sample is one of those made by
Maudie and Betty Wooding for their
order book. You will see that they
have made a mistake between the two
heads. The sample is in a fine linen
about 80 thickness.

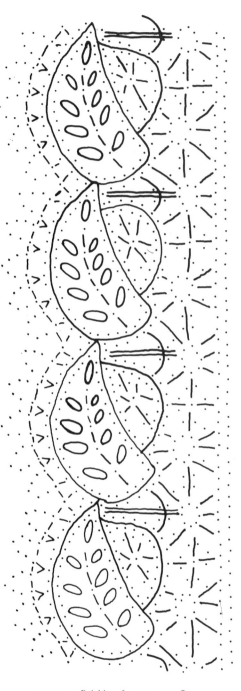

This Bedford Maltese handkerchief
edging with its elaborate corner must
have been a pattern that Lizzie
Wooding purchased and never used.
We have no sample of it and the
pricking has no sign of wear and still
bears its purchase price of 2/6d. The
Woodings bought a lot of their lace
requirements by mail order from E.P.
Rose of Bedford, whose shop has since
been taken over by a department store
chain.

The nine-pin edge variation is
similar to that on the leaf pattern 16,
chapter 4.

FIG 75. *Pricking for pattern 22* Lucy

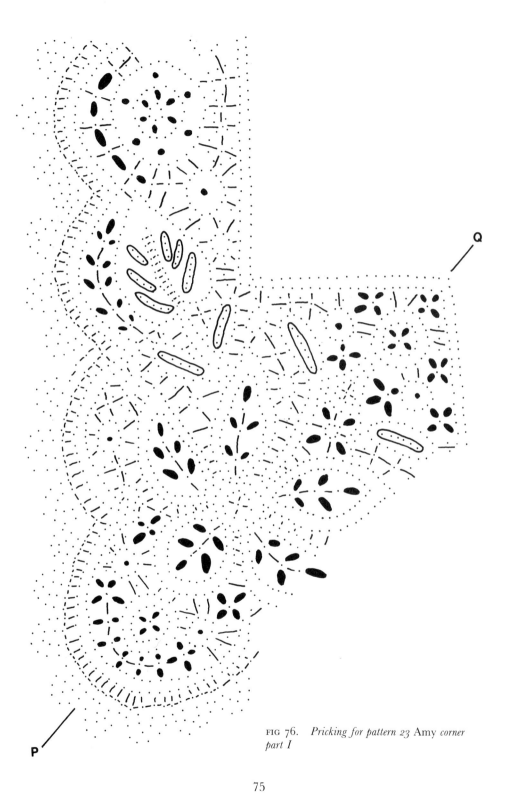

Q

P

FIG 76. *Pricking for pattern 23* Amy *corner part I*

75

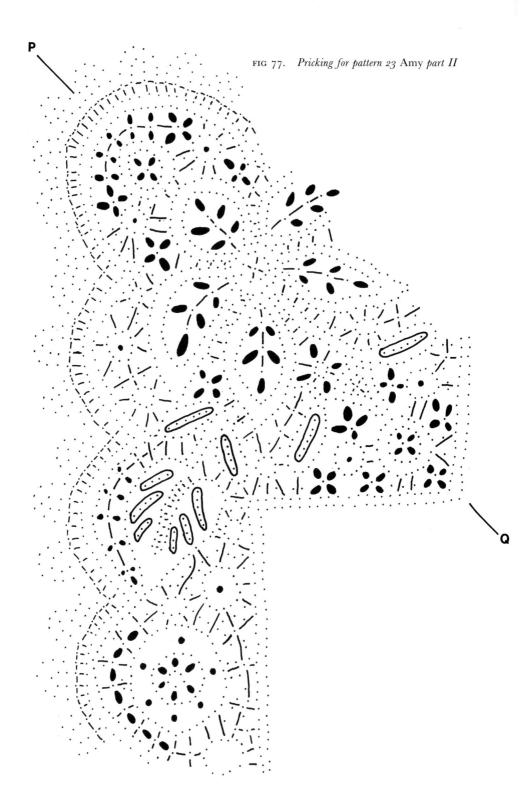

FIG 77. *Pricking for pattern 23* Amy *part II*

P

Q

FIG 78. *Catalogue from E.P. Rose of Bedford*

FIG 79. *Pattern 24* Sophia *edging with corner*

Pattern twenty-four – *Sophia* (edging with corner)

This handkerchief edging is one of those in the Bucks Cottage Worker's Agency catalogue. There it is described as the 'Fan Corner design handkerchief made up with best lawn 3/3d to 3/6d each'

The lace illustrated here was left on the pillow of Lizzie Wooding when she died and was completed by her daughter Betty. It shows the traditional way of mounting a handkerchief for presentation.

The original pricking has the words '5 heads for each side' written on it.

78

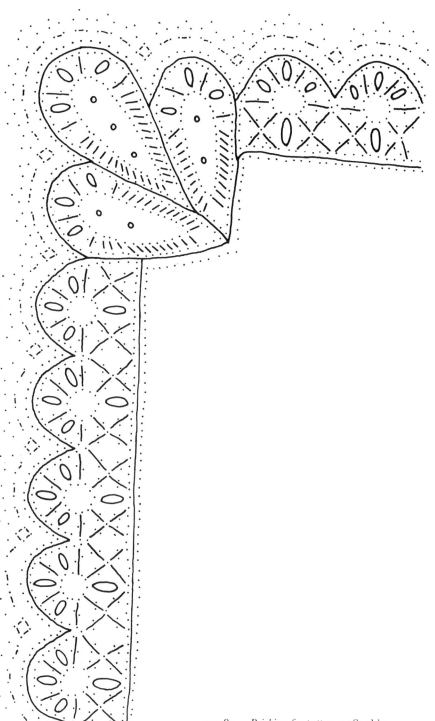

FIG 80. *Pricking for pattern 24* Sophia

79

FIG 81. *Pattern 25* Emeley *edging with corner*

Pattern twenty-five – *Emeley* (edging
with corner)
The spelling of the name of this
pattern comes from an old bobbin. It is
by far the most worn of all the patterns
in this collection and the only one that
has needed any 'trueing'. It was
obviously a very popular design.

The sample is in silk on a silk centre
and was made by Hannah Baker.

FIG 82. *Pricking for pattern 25* Emeley

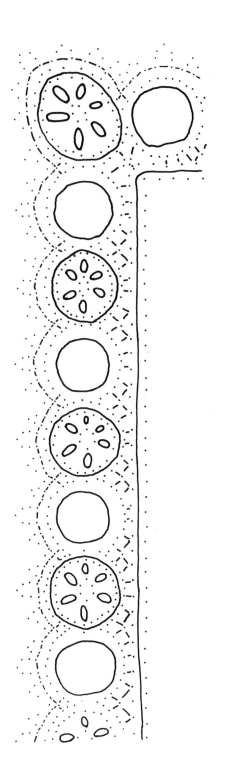

FIG 83.   *Pattern 26* Jeanne *narrow edging with corner*

Pattern twenty-six – *Jeanne* (edging with corner)

The edging in the sample was made by Lizzie Wooding and again shows the traditional way of presenting a handkerchief. The centre of the pattern is worked as follows:

Make a windmill with the braid and tally, putting up a pin in the centre. With the resulting left-hand pair and the workers from the trail make a false tally finishing with the weaver on the left. With the right-hand pair of this tally make a whole stitch with the next pair in the centre.

With the right-hand pair from the centre make a false tally with the workers from the footbraid, leaving the weaver on the right. Take the left-hand pair through two pairs in the centre and then make a braid with the other centre pair out to the trail. Finally with the other two pairs make a tally.

Two extra pairs are needed for the corner.

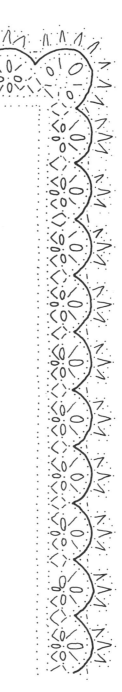

FIG 84. *Pricking for pattern 26* Jeanne

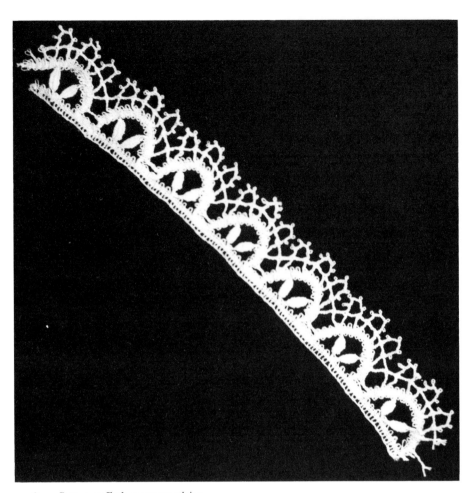

FIG 85. *Pattern 27* Esther *narrow edging*

Pattern twenty-seven – *Esther*
(edging)
A delicate little Bedford Maltese
edging of the kind used to trim
handkerchiefs and underwear. Its
rather unusual feature is the way that
the trail becomes part of the footbraid.
I made the lace in the sample using 14
pairs of 100 thickness Swedish linen. I
used the modern way of making tallies
as I felt it suited this particular
pattern.

84

FIG 86. *Pricking for pattern 27* Esther

FIG 87. *Pattern 28* Joanne *insertion*

Pattern twenty-eight – *Joanne*
(insertion)
Wide Bedford Maltese edgings like this
were often used as hatbands. There are
two samples showing slightly different
ways of working the pattern. The top
piece has square-ended tallies and no
picots on the edging – the pin is put in
the centre of the braid to hold it out in
a loop. The other version has picots
and also uses false tallies, presumably
for speed.

FIG 88.   *Pricking for pattern 28* Joanne

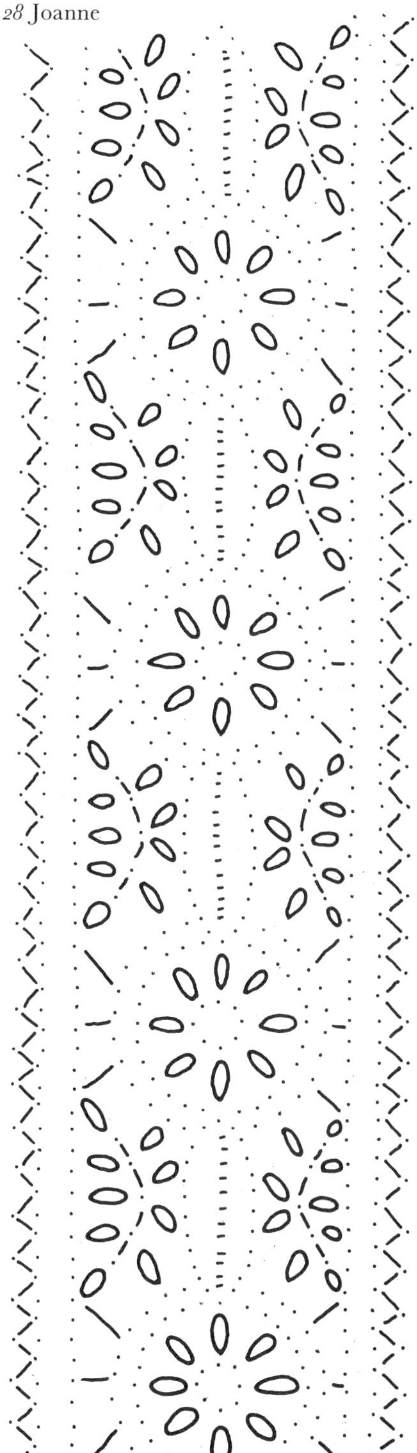

Pattern twenty-nine – *Caroline* (insertion)

There is a mixture of Bucks Point and Bedford Maltese techniques in this pattern. Often these insertions were sewn together to make whole blouses or children's dresses of lace. The sample is made in a fine silky ecru thread. I do not know for sure who made it, but she must have been annoyed to realise that she had missed one of the centre tallies.

FIG 89.   *Pattern 29* Caroline *insertion*

FIG 90.   *Pricking for pattern 29* Caroline

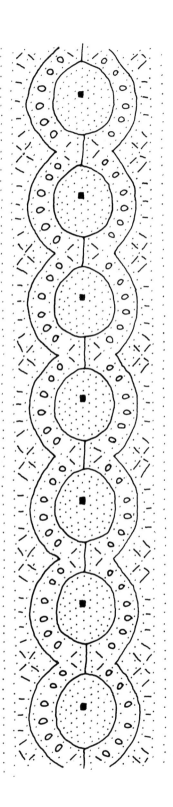

Pattern thirty – *Elizabeth* (insertion)
This is a Bedford Maltese insertion.
Like the two previous examples this
one is made in a fine silky ecru thread.
These insertions were frequently sewn
together to make complete articles of
clothing such as camisoles or blouses.
The idea was that when you were tired
of the garment you could carefully
dismantle the lace and use it for
another purpose. I have a pair of lace
cuffs in this pattern.

Note again the use of false tallies for
speed, although all the picots are
double ones.

FIG 91. *Pattern 30* Elizabeth *insertion*

90

FIG 92. *Pricking for pattern 30* Elizabeth

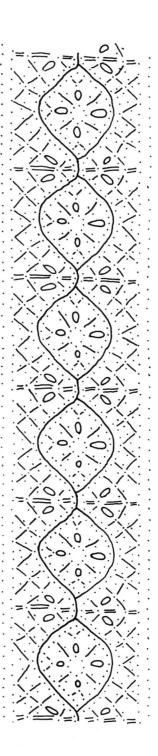

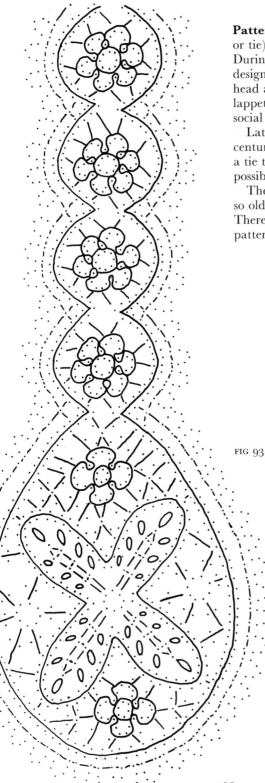

Pattern thirty-one – *Fanny* (lappett or tie)

During the mid-nineteenth century this design would have been worked on the head as a lappett. The longer your lappett tails were, the higher was your social standing.

Later, around the turn of the century, this would have been used as a tie to be worn round the neck, possibly fixed with a cameo brooch.

The original parchment pricking is so old that all the marking has faded. There should be 19 repeats of the pattern between the two ends.

FIG 93. *Pricking for pattern 31* Fanny *tie*

FOUR

THE AUNTIES' PATTERNS

(17 Torchon and other patterns)

This is a mixed bag of patterns being those originally belonging to Maudie and Betty Wooding. Although I always called them my aunts, they were actually my mother's cousins. The patterns are Torchon designs in the main but also included are some they designed themselves.

Betty Wooding was a dressmaker by profession and often made lace to trim her dresses. By far the most popular articles were modesty vests used to fill in the necklines of low-cut dresses. These were sometimes especially designed or more often lengths of lace mounted on material. They would be attached to the dresses by little gold safety pins or snap fasteners.

Other favourite patterns were motifs, either sewn into the article of clothing or attached as separate decorative features.

Maudie and Betty also made lace to trim household linen such as traycloths, tablecloths and dressing-table sets.

The majority of these designs are from the 1920s, 30s and 40s.

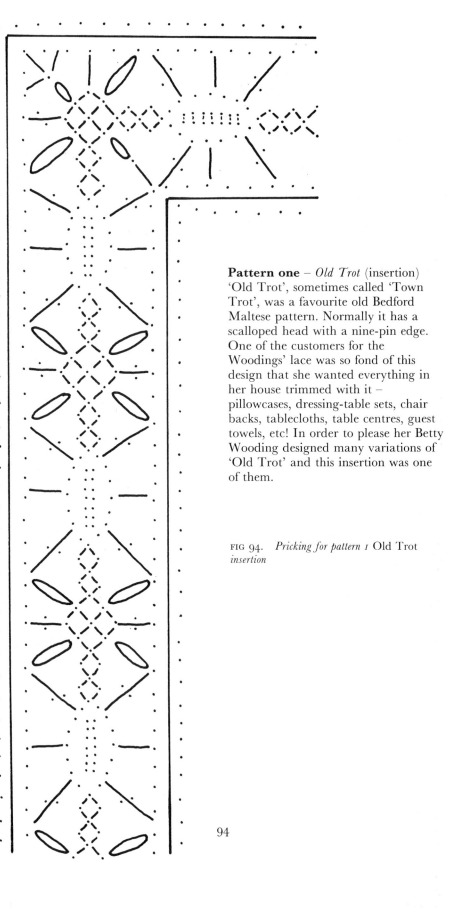

Pattern one – *Old Trot* (insertion)
'Old Trot', sometimes called 'Town
Trot', was a favourite old Bedford
Maltese pattern. Normally it has a
scalloped head with a nine-pin edge.
One of the customers for the
Woodings' lace was so fond of this
design that she wanted everything in
her house trimmed with it –
pillowcases, dressing-table sets, chair
backs, tablecloths, table centres, guest
towels, etc! In order to please her Betty
Wooding designed many variations of
'Old Trot' and this insertion was one
of them.

FIG 94. *Pricking for pattern 1* Old Trot
insertion

94

FIG 95. *Pattern 2* Maud *wide edging with corner*

Pattern two – *Maud* (edging with corner)
This wide edging with its nine-pin edge and rose ground is a mixture of Bedford Maltese and Torchon techniques. It must have been particularly popular for tablecloth edgings for the pricking is marked – '17 heads for a square yard, 22 for 1¼ square.' The finished tablecloth in the photograph is in fact 45in × 45in.

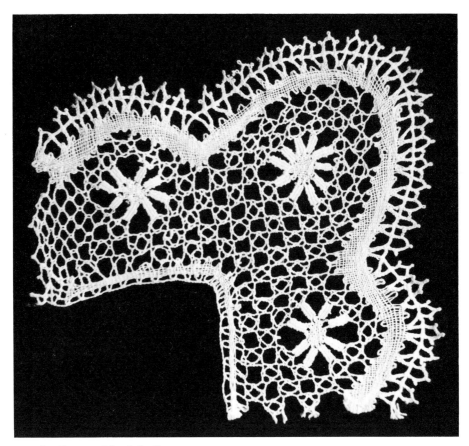

FIG 96. *Pattern 2* Maud *detail*

The lace sample was one of those made by Betty and Maudie Wooding for their customers. At the beginning they have made the common mistake of those starting up rose ground, that is, forgetting the extra stitch and twist.

FIG 97. *Pricking for pattern 2* Maud

FIG 98. *Pattern 3* Winifred *edging*

Pattern three – *Winifred* (edging)
Another wide edging with elements of
both Bedford Maltese and Torchon
lace. These patterns would have been
used largely for home furnishings. The
sample was made in old crochet cotton
called Arderns no. 14 and took 28
pairs. It is a good pattern for beginners
to try raised tallies.

This is the traditional marking for
rose ground, rather than the more up-
to-date square symbols.

FIG 99. *Pricking for pattern 3* Winifred

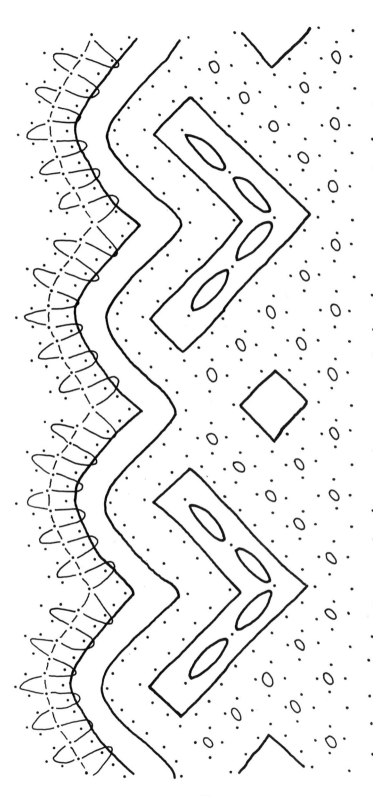

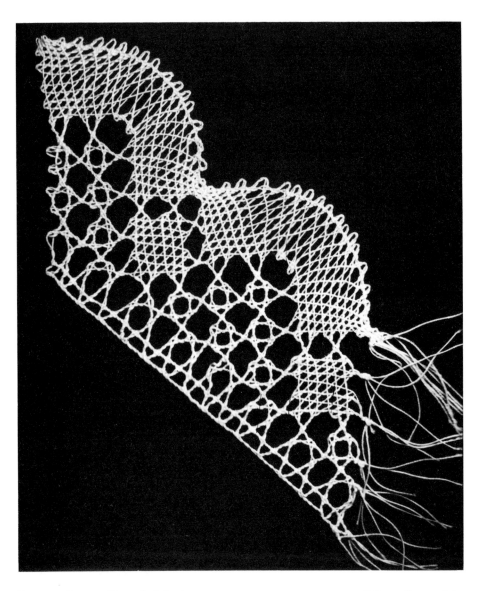

Pattern four – *Peggy* (edging)
A bold simple Torchon edging using
rose ground and half stitch. The
sample is in 25 linen. The half stitch
has a whole stitch edge except where it
goes straight into the rose ground. The
majority of these wide edgings must
originally have been made in ecru or
black thread as the prickings are
nearly all on white card.

FIG 100.   *Pattern 4* Peggy *edging*

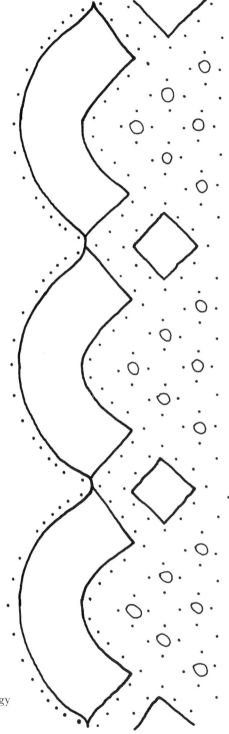

FIG 101. *Pricking for pattern 4* Peggy

FIG 102. *Pattern 5* Hazel *edging*

Pattern five – *Hazel* (edging)
Another wide edging with features of
both Torchon and Bedford Maltese
lace. In the sample 2-ply wool is used
in two colours, brown and dark blue.
The trail is in half stitch and the
colours alternate in the tallies, both
raised and flat.

Notice that although the pricking
appears to indicate a braid and tallies
crossing in the centre with an eight
pair crossing, in the actual sample the
line is just one pair twisted and the
centre is worked in whole stitch.

FIG 103. *Pricking for pattern 5* Hazel

FIG 104. *Pattern 6* Josephine *edging*

Pattern six – *Josephine* (edging)
Asymmetric designs like this seem to
have been fashionable in the 1920s and
30s. This wide one has a great variety
of techniques, combining both Bedford
Maltese and Torchon features. Notice
the slightly unusual variation to the
nine-pin edge.

There was no sample of this lace in
the collection so I made this one. It
took 42 pairs in 50 Swedish linen.

FIG 105. *Pricking for pattern 6* Josephine

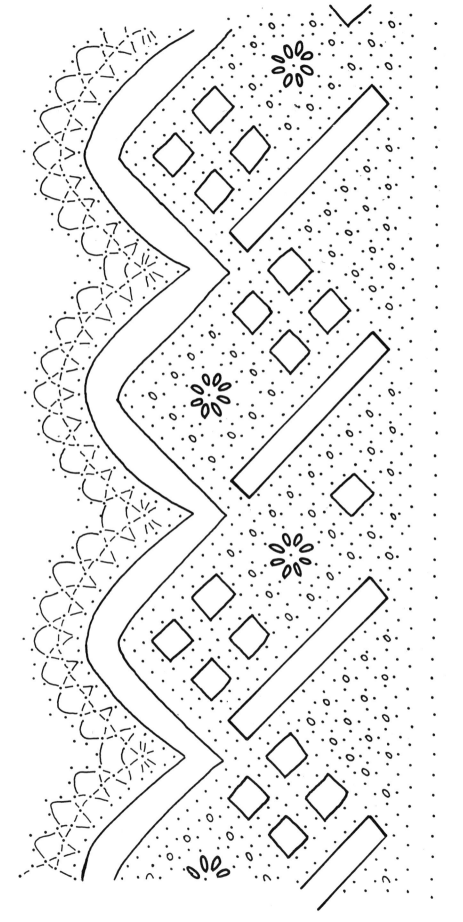

FIG 106. *Pattern 7* Clair *edging*

Pattern seven – *Clair* (edging)
A wide Torchon edging that would
have been used to trim household
linen. There is an unusual feature in
the scalloped head, giving it a two-tier
effect – just follow the lines to work it.
This is another pattern suitable for
beginners at raised tallies. These rolled
ones were often kept in place with a
match-stick whilst working.

The sample was made in an old
crochet cotton called Arderns no. 14,
about equivalent to a modern 20
cotton.

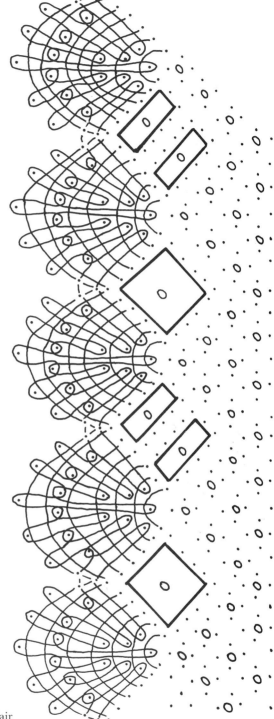

FIG 107.   *Pricking for pattern 7* Clair

107

FIG 108. *Pattern 8* Eleanor *edging*

Pattern eight – *Eleanor* (edging)
There are a couple of intriguing
features about this Torchon pattern.
First, although the sample has a
corner, there is no pricking in the
collection with one. So I leave the
lacemaker to work it out for herself.

Secondly, whoever made the sample
has a rather unusual way of working
rose ground. I can only come to the
conclusion that she wasn't very good at
it as there is one example of the more
usual method of working in the corner
head.

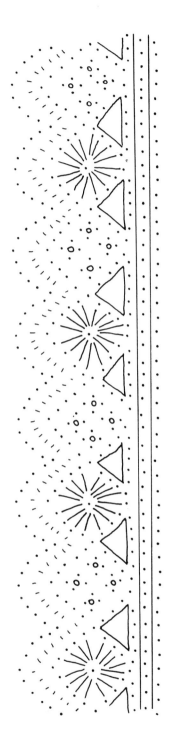

FIG 109. *Pricking for pattern 8* Eleanor

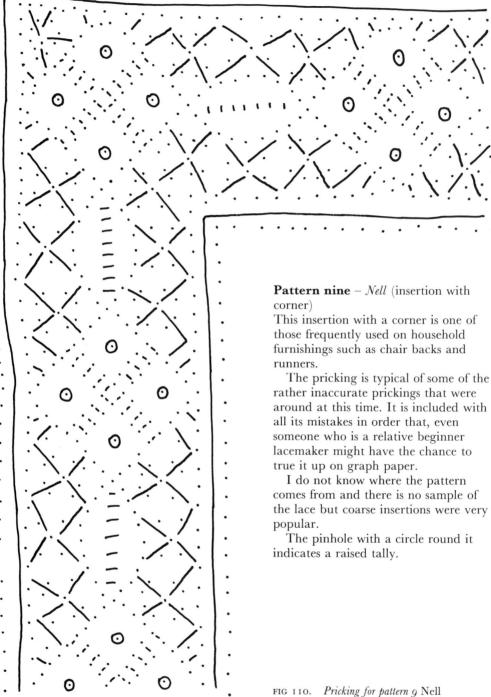

Pattern nine – *Nell* (insertion with corner)

This insertion with a corner is one of those frequently used on household furnishings such as chair backs and runners.

The pricking is typical of some of the rather inaccurate prickings that were around at this time. It is included with all its mistakes in order that, even someone who is a relative beginner lacemaker might have the chance to true it up on graph paper.

I do not know where the pattern comes from and there is no sample of the lace but coarse insertions were very popular.

The pinhole with a circle round it indicates a raised tally.

FIG 110. *Pricking for pattern 9* Nell

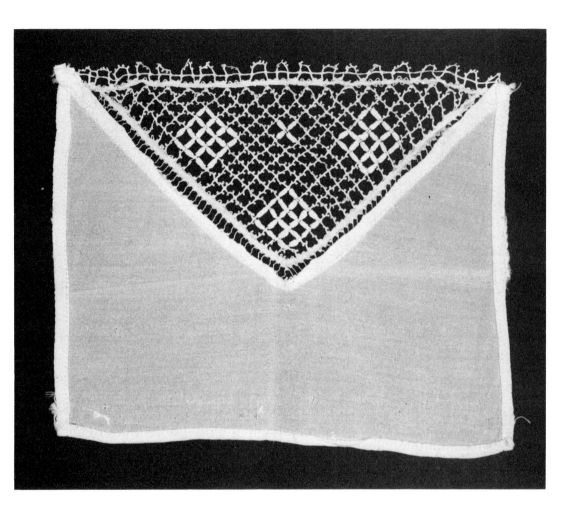

FIG 111. *Pattern 10* Betty

Pattern ten – *Betty* (corner or modesty vest)
This is a design by Betty Wooding for a modesty vest. She often worked them as accessories for the dresses that she made. She was particularly fond of tallies and picots in her designs.

The pattern could equally be used as a handkerchief corner.

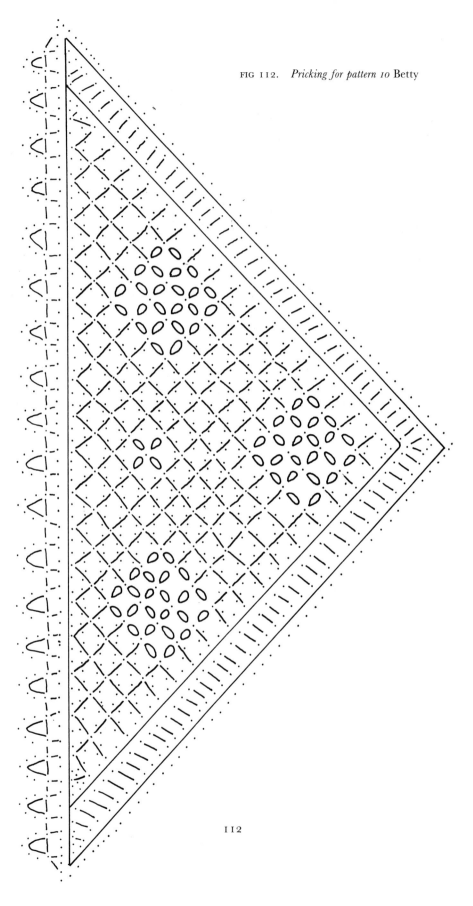

FIG 112. *Pricking for pattern 10* Betty

FIG 113. *Pattern 11* Charlotte *modesty vest or corner*

Pattern eleven – *Charlotte* (corner or modesty vest)
I believe that this was another of Betty Wooding's designs. The lace is made in a fine silky thread and mounted on silk. The pricking is marked – modesty vest no. 5, 3/6d.

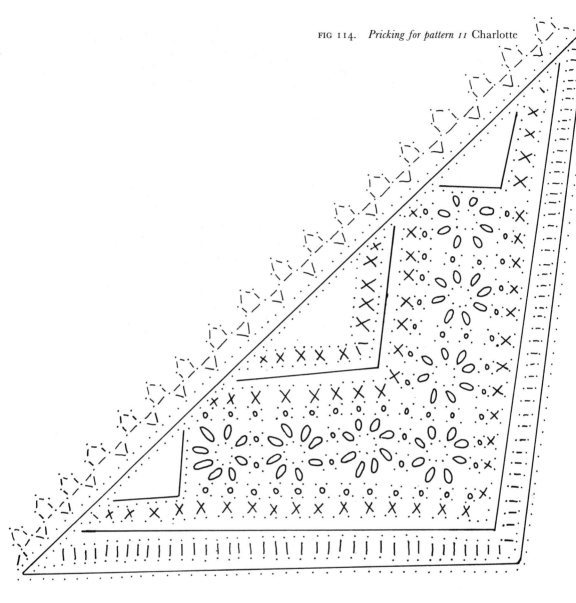

FIG 114. *Pricking for pattern 11* Charlotte

Pattern twelve – *Elsie* (corner)

This is an old pattern for a corner that Betty Wooding later redesigned as a modesty vest. This, however, is the original corner design which could possibly be a piece of Continental lace as the tallies all have pointed ends rather than the English square ones despite the fact that it is an old piece of lace.

In the centre the lines are made with single pairs and there is no pin hole where they cross. Where there is a pin hole it is therefore a six-pair crossing with the tallies as well.

114

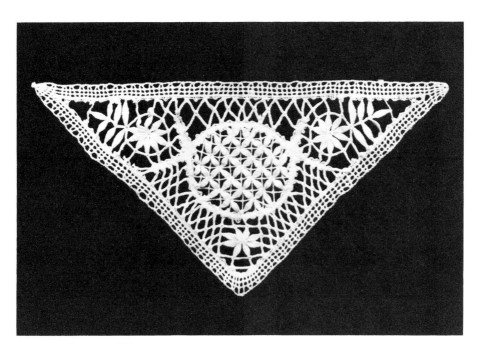

FIG 115. *Pattern 12* Elsie *modesty vest or corner*

FIG 116. *Pricking for pattern 12* Elsie

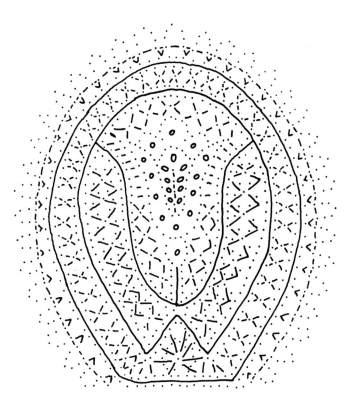

FIG 117. *Pricking for pattern 13* Penelope *motif*

Pattern thirteen – *Penelope* (motif)
Betty Wooding designed a great many of these petal shapes. They could be inserted into blouses and dresses or more usually four would be made and gathered together into a flower for a buttonhole on a dress lapel.

This particular design is based on the pattern in the collar pattern 7, chapter 2.

There is no sample of the lace, but I hope that experienced lacemakers will feel tempted to try it for themselves.

FIG 118. *Pattern 14* Petal *motif*

FIG 119. *Pricking for pattern 14* Petal

Pattern fourteen – *Petal* (motif)
This is another of Betty Wooding's
petal designs. The original pricking is
drawn out in pencil on a thin piece of
paper with the starting point indicated.

I think that this pattern was
definitely intended to be made up into
a flower and starched. Nowadays fine
wire can be used in place of one of the
passives to give extra rigidity.

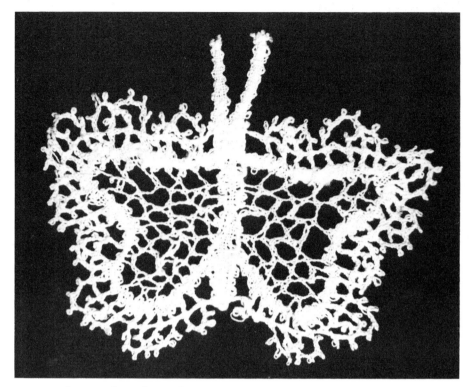

FIG 120. *Pattern 15* Butterfly *motif*

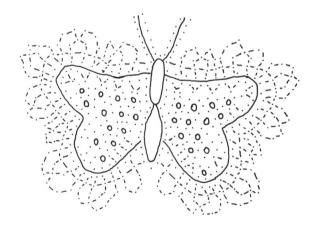

FIG 121. *Pricking for pattern 15* Butterfly

Pattern fifteen – *Butterfly* (motif)
This is very similar to a design in the Bucks Cottage Workers' Agency catalogue where it is described as a butterfly medallion, priced at 9d each. There the filling is definitely honeycomb, on the pricking it is indicated as rose ground; whereas whoever made the sample – possibly an elderly Lizzie Wooding seems completely undecided!

I have included the pattern in this section because Betty Wooding used them for her dressmaking.

The work is started at the bottom finishing at the end of the antennae.

Pattern sixteen – *Leaf* (motif)
This is yet another pattern which is
very similar to one in the Bucks
Cottage Workers' Agency catalogue.
However, the nine-pin edge is different
and there are less tallies in the
catalogue version. When the catalogue
came out they were charging 8½d for
this piece of lace, about 20 years later
the Wooding sisters asked 1/- for it.

The leaf would have decorated
blouses and dresses. There are various
samples in the collection made in both
linen and silk.

The work should commence at the
top of the leaf, finishing with the stem.
In this fine lace the raised tallies would
be temporarily supported with a thick
pin rather than the matchstick used in
coarser work.

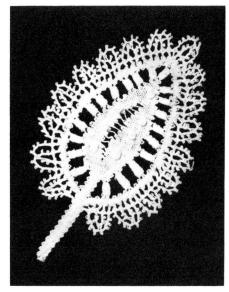

FIG 122.   *Pattern 16* Leaf *motif*

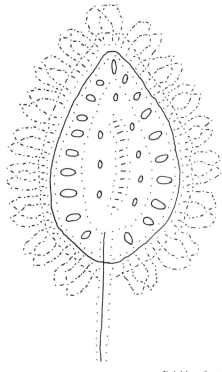

FIG 123.   *Pricking for pattern 16* Leaf

Pattern seventeen – *Basket* (motif)
Many patterns for tablecloth, traycloth
or even dress insertions were taken
from everyday objects. I believe that
this basket was one of Betty Wooding's
designs. The original is made in a fine
linen.

The work starts in the bottom right-
hand corner, working upwards around
the edge of the basket.

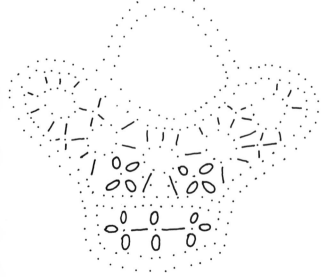

KATIE BAGLEY'S PATTERNS

(3 mystery patterns)

Maudie and Betty were still making lace at a time when the craft had almost disappeared, this meant that they often received lacemaking equipment from the families of lacemakers who had died. Frequently they knew very little about the lacemaker herself.

One of these lacemakers was Katie Bagley. Almost all her patterns have her name on them and her Continental-style bobbins have K.B. scorched into the thick end.

Who she was I am afraid we do not know. It seems quite likely that she was French. Among her patterns are many DMC Torchon ones, obviously professionally produced. Other patterns have the number of 'fuseaux' needed written on them.

Maybe she married an Englishman and came to live here. The little hand-made catalogue of the Rose Belle Lace Industry dated 1915 *(see Fig. 15)* came with her collection. The prices are in shillings and cents – whether this means centimes we do not know for sure.

The following patterns were originally hand pricked out and the markings drawn in with a fine pen. Two of them are in red ink, all of them on pink cardboard.

There are no lace samples in the collection for these patterns but lacemakers might like to try to work them out for themselves.

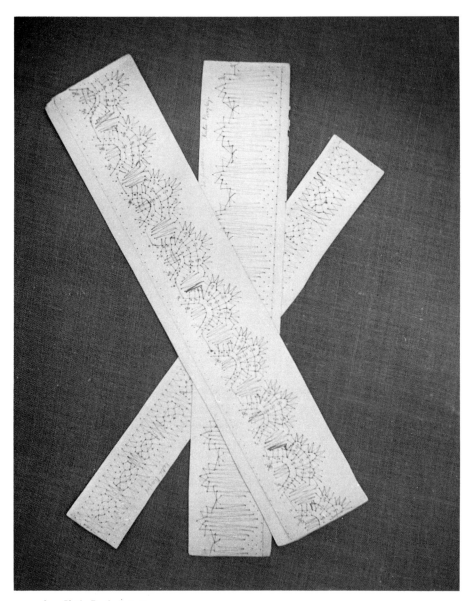

FIG 126. *Katie Bagley's patterns*

Pattern one – *Katie* (insertion)
A neat little insertion drawn out and
possibly even designed by Katie
Bagley. I think that the circle round
the pin hole indicates a picot.

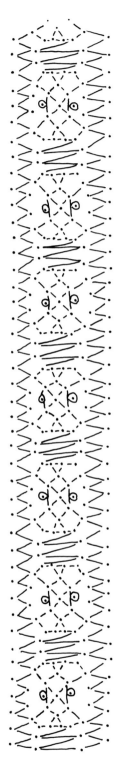

FIG 127. *Pricking for pattern 1* Katie *insertion*

123

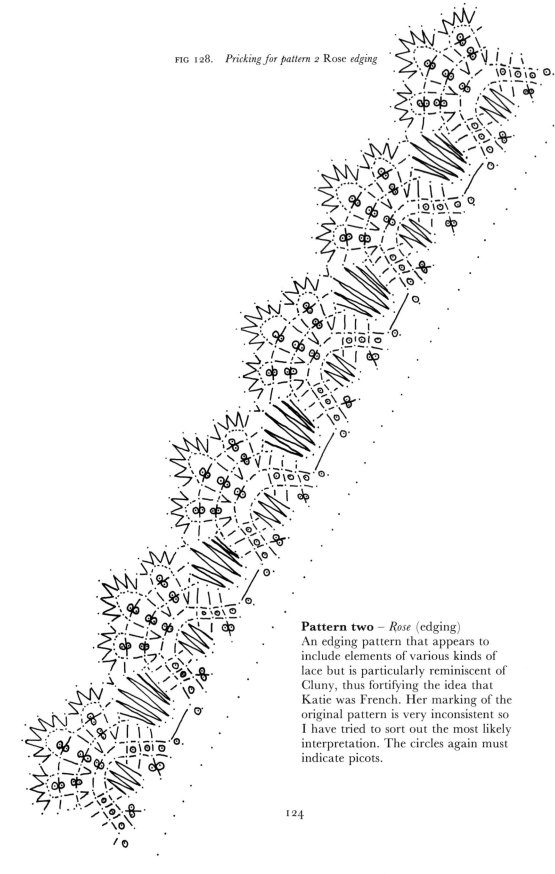

FIG 128. *Pricking for pattern 2 Rose edging*

Pattern two – *Rose* (edging)
An edging pattern that appears to
include elements of various kinds of
lace but is particularly reminiscent of
Cluny, thus fortifying the idea that
Katie was French. Her marking of the
original pattern is very inconsistent so
I have tried to sort out the most likely
interpretation. The circles again must
indicate picots.

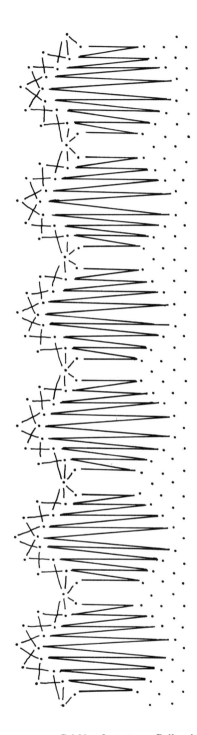

Pattern three – *Belle* (edging)
This really is an intriguing pattern, not
so much as to how it should be worked
as to what it was used for. My only
guess is a heavy lace for trimming
household linen.

This is the only one of these patterns
that states the required number of
bobbins – 36 fuseaux. It is interesting
that she gives the number of individual
bobbins rather than pairs.

FIG 129. *Pricking for pattern 3* Belle *edging*

SIX

MY PATTERNS

(5 modern patterns)

When I was 11 years old I went to spend a week with Aunty Maudie and Aunty Betty, at their request, in order that they could teach me to make lace. They wanted the tradition to be carried on in the family.

I still have the first thing I made; a handkerchief with nine-pin edging. I learnt the basic principles of Bedford Maltese lace and a little about Torchon. Whenever I visited them I would discuss various problems and they also sent me a series of lessons by post. Thus my knowledge of lace was built up.

My earliest attempts at designing were very similar to Aunty Betty's – a great many braids and tallies. I also worked out variations on traditional patterns.

The following five patterns have all been designed within the last five years; I usually find that I have to have a definite project in mind and then it is easier to work out an actual pattern. In this case I decided to make a curtain.

Curtain
After one of my students had very successfully designed a tablecloth for herself I thought that I would like to try my hand at something similar. We had just moved into a new house and I decided to make a lace curtain for the window of the back door.

I designed and worked a strip at a time until I reached the centre and then repeated the first two strips to balance up the pattern. A great deal of Torchon ground was included in order to let in as much light as possible. The little strip of 'V' shapes was part of each individual strip in the curtain, but here I have separated it to make a bookmark.

The strips were joined on the pillow with Honiton sewings on the left-hand side. I used a Belgian linen thread no. 50, with the passives in an ecru crochet cotton to give a Regency stripe effect.

The finished curtain was folded over at the top to make a single hem, tacked with the same linen thread and hung from a length of curtain wire. It is 66cm wide by 86cm long. As can be seen, the threads were left at the bottom and cut to form a fringe.

FIG 130. *The complete curtain*

Pattern one – *Rachel* (wide insertion)
This is the centre strip and the most
complicated of the curtain patterns.

The ground within the gimps is
Swedish Brabant ground (half stitch,
pin, half stitch, twist at each pin hole).
The heart shape can be done in half or
whole stitch, according to personal
preference. I alternated them in the
curtain. It is advisable when dropping
pairs out as the heart narrows to take
each pair through the gimp and work
the first pin hole of the Torchon
ground. This stabilises the heart shape
and reduces the risk of taking out too
many pairs at a time.

One repeat of the pattern is
indicated by the arrows. Forty pairs of
linen thread are used. One pair on
each of the outside pinholes and two
pairs on all the others.

Eight pairs of passives in a
contrasting thread are needed, four to
each outside pinhole. There is one
main pair of gimps and two subsidiary
pairs, although it is possible by
working one side of the design at a
time to make do with only one extra
pair. I found that a double gimp
thread showed up more clearly.

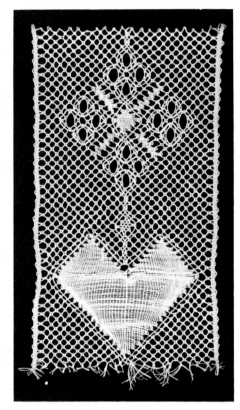

FIG 131.   *Pattern 1* Rachel *wide insertion*

FIG 132.   *Pricking for pattern 1* Rachel

Pattern two – *Michael* (bookmark)
This pattern is based on the design in
the narrow band between each of the
stripes in the curtain. The stripes are
whole and half stitch alternated. The
effect is perhaps more masculine than
some lace bookmarks.

Sixteen pairs of a fine linen thread
are used and a total of 11 pairs of a
slightly coarser contrast thread.

The most convenient way to start is
to turn the work upside down and
hang two pairs of the main thread,
twisted, at the pin hole marked *x*. Lay
ten pairs of the contrast thread across
the pillow below the pin. Take the
right-hand pair of the main thread
through the contrast threads in whole
stitches, that is five complete stitches.
Put in a pin at *1* and return in whole
stitch to the inside of the work. Take
the other pair from *x* out to *2* and back
in a similar fashion. Then turn the
pillow round the normal way and start
adding the other pairs at each inside
pin hole.

After completing the first stripe twist
all the main colour pairs and take the
final contrast thread as a gimp through
all the main colour pairs except the
outside workers. This gimp then joins
the passive threads down the sides and
one thread only is thrown out from each
side.

At the finish of the bookmark the
pairs are cut off about an inch below
the work to make a fringe.

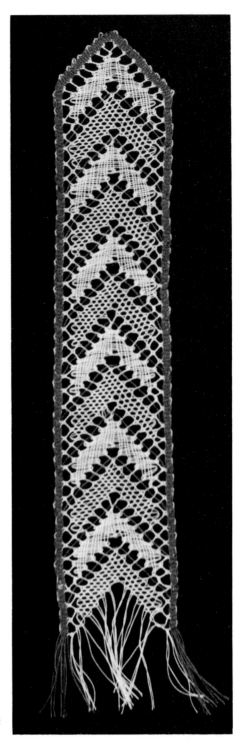

FIG 133. *Pattern 2* Michael *bookmark*

FIG 134. *Pricking for pattern 2* Michael

FIG 135. *Pattern 3* Valerie *wide insertion*

Pattern three – *Valerie* (wide insertion)

This insertion was designed as part of the lace curtain so a good deal of Torchon ground was used in order to let in as much light as practicable. In the curtain the design is alternately worked in whole and half stitch, but many variations of this are possible.

The pattern needs 40 pairs of a thread about the coarseness of no. 50 linen, and eight extra pairs for the passives at the sides, which can be in the same or a contrasting thread.

FIG 136. *Pricking for pattern 3* Valerie   133

FIG 137. *Pattern 4* Stanley *wide insertion*

Pattern four – *Stanley* (wide insertion)
This design is complementary to the previous one and was also designed with the intention of letting in the maximum amount of light.

Once again the original pattern was worked in whole stitch and half stitch by turns, but could be done in any number of variations.

This pattern, too, requires 40 pairs for the main part with eight pairs for the passives at the sides. Swedish linen no. 50 is about the right thickness.

FIG 138. *Pricking for pattern 4* Stanley

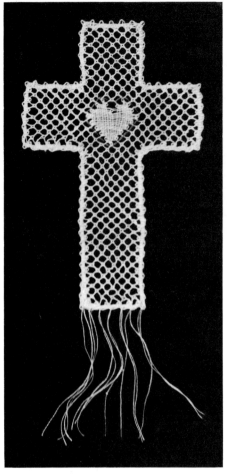

FIG 139.   *Pattern 5* Gorsehill *bookmark*

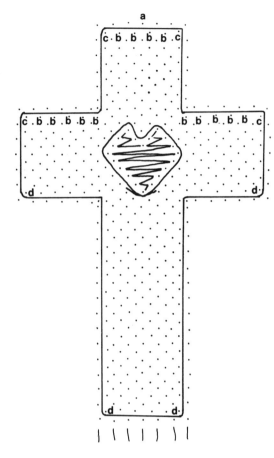

FIG 140.   *Pricking for pattern 5* Gorsehill

Pattern five – *Gorsehill* (bookmark)
This little bookmark was designed to be used in a Bible. It illustrates the text 'God so loved the world, that He gave His only begotten Son, that whosoever believeth in Him should not perish, but have everlasting life' – John 3, verse 16.

The most convenient starting point is *a*. Hang two pairs here for workers. Lie eight pairs across as passives. Add two pairs at each point marked *b* and one pair at points marked *c*. Take out pairs in the trail opposite. It is possible to complete one side of the cross and use the pairs taken out on the other side. The ground is Torchon ground.

The heart shape stands out best in cloth stitch. The gimp round it looks particularly effective in a metallic thread such as gold or silver.

Blind pairs are worked at points *c* and *d*. Finish at one of the corners at the bottom, dropping off pairs for a fringe.

136

SEVEN

TRADITIONAL TIPS

Always use a worker cloth underneath the bobbins and fold it up over the lace when you stop working for however short a time. When making a large piece of lace remember to wash the worker cloth frequently.

When pricking out a pattern always use a pricker finer than the pins to be used in working the lace. This makes sure that the pins hold firm when you make the lace.

Try to keep all working bobbins level. This improves the tension. The ideal distance is for the head of the bobbin to be approximately a bobbin's length away from the work.

If, when you are undoing the lace to rectify a mistake, you have to leave the work for any reason, put a pin (preferably a colour-headed one) in a prominent place by itself in the pricking. This should help to remind you to carry on undoing on your return. It is very frustrating to discover that you have got to undo something twice!

When you have finished a piece of lace do not remove it from the pillow immediately. Leave the pins in for a while in order to consolidate the work.

It is traditional to have one button amongst the spangles on your pillow.

Do make gimp threads noticeable. They should be too thick, rather than too fine when they would not be seen at all.

When making the slip knot to hold the thread on the bobbin, twist it round a couple of extra times to counteract the tendency of the knot to slip. Aunty Maudie told me that this used to be called 'elshing' a bobbin, but she was not sure how to spell it.

Keep lace stored in blue or black tissue paper. This helps to prevent it turning yellow. If possible, roll it rather than fold it to prevent creases forming.

A simple way to dye a piece of white lace to a delicate pinky-brown shade is to soak it overnight in cold tea.

When working a stitch always give a very slight tug on the threads to pull them up into place. With fine threads, this, of course, must be done very carefully.

Try to discipline yourself to keep a sample book. It will prove invaluable for checking on the working of a pattern, and also show you how your work has improved.

It is a good idea occasionally to twist the passives in the footbraid, especially on a long piece of work or when going round a corner. It helps stop the tendency of the threads to pucker.

When starting a piece of lace, work about two inches before starting to remove the pins from the back and using them again.

If interrupted during the making of a tally lay the weaving thread over the back of the pillow amongst the pins. Then it will not slip down and pull the tally out of shape.

A professional Victorian lacemaker would often leave the knots in her thread. It is amazing how they disappear into the lace. However, nowadays we prefer to make a neater join by attaching a full bobbin to a nearby pin and working the threads double for as many pinholes as possible.

When throwing pairs out of a trail for any reason always use a middle pair, never the outside ones.

After cutting off bobbins from a finished piece of lace, put them in a bag or box and immediately label it with the type and thickness of thread. It can be very difficult to recognise the thread later.

Whatever kind of bobbin winder you use, try to handle the thread as little as possible.

It was traditional in the east Midlands to use colour-headed pins on the head and footside of the lace. If beads were too expensive, pickled goosegrass seed-heads were pushed on the pin-heads, and also sealing wax.

The pins on the footside should be put in to lean out at a slight angle to take the strain. An extra twist should also be used on the outside pair of bobbins for the same reason.

Bran used in the stuffing of a pincushion helps to keep the pins clean, and lavender or some other herb makes it smell nice too. A traditional one would be heart-shaped.

Try to find a really comfortable lacemaking chair. It should have a high straight back. A little cushion tied on at the top is a good idea. The occupational hazard of lacemaking was curvature of the spine rather than blindness.

Do not keep a straw-filled pillow in a plastic bag or a warm place when not in use. It can be a shock to discover that unsuspected tiny eggs have hatched out in the extra warmth.

Always use a plain dark colour for your pillow. It is more restful on the eyes. The material should be as smooth as possible. Threads from a fluffy material can get worked into the lace. For the same reason be careful not to comb your hair near the pillow!

When you have finished working a piece of lace, write suggestions regarding number of bobbins, stitches used etc., on the pricking before putting it away. It may help you or another lacemaker in the dim and distant future.

GLOSSARY

I have presumed that readers already know the basic principles of lacemaking. This is just an explanation of some of the terms they may not have come across before.

Bedford Maltese lace Developed in the east Midlands during the nineteenth century. Slightly coarser than Buckinghamshire Point lace its designs were reminiscent of Maltese lace. Also called English Maltese lace

Blind pin A pinhole that is used twice when working a curve in a trail

Braids Made by plaiting four threads in a continuous series of half stitches. Also called brides, legs and plaits

Buckinghamshire Point lace The lace originally made in the east Midlands area. It is a fine lace with a net ground and the pattern outlined with a gimp thread

Bud Any feature of a lace pattern which cannot be distinguished by any other name, that is it is not a ground, tally or trail

Cloth stitch A continuous section in whole stitch

Cucumber (See false tally)

Eight pair crossing Work as follows: Regard each pair as a single thread
1) Work a half-stitch with the centre four pairs
2) Work a half stitch with the right-hand four pairs
3) Work a half stitch with the left-hand four pairs
4) Repeat all three half stitches
5) Put in a pin
6) Work a whole stitch with the centre four pairs
7) Cross the sixth pair over the seventh
8) Cross the second over the third
9) Pull up into position

False tally A tally made between two sections of lace by using a pair from either side. Sometimes called a cucumber

Foot, footside The straight edge of a piece of lace. The side that joins on to a piece of material. In English lace it is always on the right-hand side of the work

Gimp thread A thicker thread woven through a pattern as the work progresses to outline a distinctive feature

Ground The background section of a lace pattern. Usually an openwork net

Head A complete repeat of a pattern

Headside The decorative side of a piece of lace that does not join on to the material. In English lace it is on the left-hand side of the work

Kiss A join between two sections of lace made by taking the workers from each side, twisting them, working a whole stitch, twisting them again and using each pair as workers to the opposite section. No pin is used

Picots Tiny loops on braids for decoration. Also used on the headside in Buckinghamshire Point lace

Raised tallies Tallies worked within a piece of whole or half stitch and raised above it. Sometimes they are rolled over and the threads re-enter the main part at the same place as they left (see pattern 7, chapter 4) or otherwise they lie flat on top and re-enter further on (see pattern 3, chapter 4)

Six pair crossing Work as follows: Regard each pair as a single thread. Numbering from the left
   1)   Take the fourth pair over the fifth
   2)   Take the third pair under the second
   3)   Cross the fourth pair over the third pair
   4)   Put in the pin
   5)   Take the fourth pair over the fifth and under the sixth
   6)   Take third pair under the second and over the first
   7)   Take the fourth pair over the fifth
   8)   Take the third pair under the second
   9)   Cross the fourth pair over the third
   10) Take the fourth pair over the fifth
   11) Take the third pair under the second
   12) Pull up into position

Tally A feature in lace where one thread is woven round the other three. English lace traditionally had square-ended ones. Also called a plait or a leaf

Torchon lace A geometric lace developed originally in France during the latter part of the nineteenth century. It became popular in this country as a beginners' lace

Trail A long narrow section of lace worked in the same stitch, usually whole stitch, but occasionally half stitch

Windmill A crossing for four pairs. Regard the pairs as single threads and work a whole stitch, putting the pin in before the last movement of the stitch

FURTHER READING

Channer, C.C., and Waller, M., *Lacemaking Point Ground*, Dryad Press

Clare, Raie, *The Dryad Book of Bobbin Lace*, Dryad Press

Collier, Ann, *Creative Design in Bobbin Lace*, Batsford

Cook, Bridget M., and Stott, Geraldine, *Batsford Book of Bobbin Lace Stitches*, Batsford

Dye, Gilian, *Beginning Bobbin Lace*, Dryad Press

Dye, Gilian, *Bobbin Lace Braid*, Batsford

Earnshaw, Pat, *Bobbin and Needlelaces: Identification and Care*, Batsford

Fisher, Jennifer, *Braid Lace for Today*, Dryad Press

Kenn, Elwyn, *Point Ground Patterns from Australia*, Dryad Press

Lovesey, Nenia, *Punto Tagliato Lace*, Dryad Press

Maidment, Margaret, *Manual of Handmade Bobbin Laces*, Batsford

Nottingham, Pamela, *Technique of Bobbin Lace*, Batsford

Nottingham, Pamela, *Bobbin Lacemaking*, Batsford

O'Cleirigh, Nellie, *Carrickmacrcoss Lace*, Dryad Press

Rowe, Veronica, *Limerick Lace*, Dryad Press

Stillwell, Alexandra, *Drafting Torchon Lace Patterns*, Dryad Press

Withers, Jean, *Mounting and Using Lace*, Dryad Press

Zwaal-Lint, Tiny, *New Bobbin Lace Patterns*, Batsford

Zwaal-Lint, Tiny, *Bobbin Lace Patterns*, Batsford

SUPPLIERS

A. Sells
'Lane Cove'
49 Pedley Lane
Clifton
Shefford
Beds
Equipment, threads and books

Mace and Nairn
89 Crane Street
Salisbury
Wilts
Threads and equipment

Sebalace
76 Main Street
Addingham
Ilkley
West Yorks
All lacemaking requisites

John & Jennifer Ford
5 Squirrels Hollow
Boney Way
Walsall
All lacemaking requisites and bobbin-maker

Shireburn Lace
Finkle Court
Finkle Hill
Sherburn in Elmet
North Yorks
Lace specialist

Teazle Embroideries
35 Boothferry Road
Hull
North Humberside
Needlepoint lace specialist

The Editor
Guild of Needlelaces
39 Napier Road
Crowthorne
Berkshire

The Lace Guild
c/o The Hollies
53 Audnam
Stourbridge
West Midlands

Deka Fabric Paints
Blythe Road
Hammersmith
London W14

Transfers
Deighton Bros Ltd
Riverside Road
Barnstaple
North Devon

Silks & Silk
Jack Piper
Silverdale
Flax Lane
Glemsford
Suffolk

The English Lace School
Honiton Court
Rockbeare
Nr Exeter
Devon
Books, threads, needles, pins, etc.

G. Hall
90 Shrewsbury Crescent
Humbledon
Tyne and Wear
Afficots, ring boxes and other fine tools

Newnham Lace Equipment
15 Marlow Close
Basingstoke
Hants

D.H. Shaw
47 Zamor Crescent
Thurcroft
Rotherham
South Yorks
Bobbin-maker

C.&D. Springett
21 Hillmorton Road
Rugby
Warwicks
CV22 5BE
Bobbin-maker

INDEX